LIBERTY DESIGN
1874-1914
BARBARA MORRIS

PYRAMID BOOKS

Overleaf: *Clock in 'Tudric' pewter by*
Archibald Knox

Above: *'The Melbury', a textile design*
by Sidney Mawson

First published in 1989 by Pyramid, an imprint of the
Octopus Publishing Group,
Michelin House, 81 Fulham Road, London SW3 6RB

Copyright © Octopus Books Limited 1989
ISBN 1 871307 71 6

Produced by Mandarin Offset

Printed and bound in Hong Kong

CONTENTS

INTRODUCTION

Arthur Lasenby Liberty, portrait by Arthur Hacker R.A., 1913

Arthur Lasenby Liberty, the founder of Liberty's, when manager of Farmer & Rogers's Oriental Warehouse, told his artist friends that if only he had a shop of his own he would change the whole look of fashion in dress and decoration. This he was to do, and some years later an article on 'The Place of the Artist in Modern Production' (*Textilia*, vol. 1, 1918–1919, p. 111), quoted a letter written to him by the distinguished architect Richard Norman Shaw (1831–1912):

Yes, you have put your mark on our time – like Pugin, Whistler, and fortunately some others. You found things, most of them beastly, and you leave them glorious in colour and full of interest. What more could you desire? It is the fashion nowadays to run down commercialism, but I don't see it – it is only when commercialism is bad, and associated with bad art, that it is objectionable; in other respects it is good and right, and a good backbone. Go on and prosper; and the longer you go on, and the more you prosper, the better for art.

Arthur Lasenby Liberty was born on 13 August 1843, in the small Buckinghamshire market town of Chesham, where his father owned a draper's shop in the High Street. When he was eight the family moved to Nottingham where his uncle had a lace warehouse. He was an exceptionally intelligent boy who showed artistic leanings at an early age, and hoped for a university education. Owing to his father's financial difficulties, however, he left school early to work briefly in his uncle's warehouse. Still only sixteen, he was sent to London to be a clerk in a wine merchant's, owned by another uncle. Unhappy in this position, he spent two further frustrating years apprenticed to a Baker Street draper, Mr John Weekes, before obtaining a post in 1862 in a more prestigious establishment in Regent Street – Farmer & Rogers' Great Shawl and Cloak Emporium. As well as selling Paisley, Norwich and French shawls, Farmer & Rogers imported woven and embroidered shawls from India and China and, at the close of the London International Exhibition of 1862, bought a considerable portion of the important Japanese exhibit. This formed the basis of their Oriental Warehouse which they opened next door to their main premises. Arthur Liberty was chosen to work there and, two years later in 1864 at the age of 21, was appointed manager.

Farmer & Rogers soon became a meeting place for artists and the devotees of 'art for art's sake'. It was also the place to buy your blue and white china. Whistler came in search of what he called his 'Long Elizas' – after the Dutch name of 'Lange Lyzen' – which were tall blue and white Chinese vases, and painters such as Albert Moore eagerly sought the soft, subtly coloured Oriental silks to drape on their models.

In an interview in *The Daily Chronicle* some fifty years later, Arthur Liberty related how 'famous artists got the idea that I took a real interest in what we sold and my knowledge and appreciation of art were extended by prolonged visits to their studios, where I was always made welcome'. He became a close friend of the actress Ellen Terry, and married an actress, Martha Cottam, on 8 June 1865, a marriage disapproved of by the family and of only brief duration. The Oriental Warehouse soon became the most successful part of the Farmer & Rogers' enterprise, and after working for them for twelve years Arthur Liberty asked to be taken into partnership. This request was refused and his artist friends encouraged him to set up on his own, promising to transfer their patronage to him. He had no capital of his own but in 1874 he became engaged to Emma Louise Blackmore, and her father put up the money to enable him to purchase the lease of a half-shop, No. 218A, Regent Street, to which he gave the grand name of East India House. It opened to the public on 15 May 1875. William Judd, who had worked with him at Farmer & Rogers, joined him as chief assistant, together with a sixteen-year-old girl, Hannah Browning, and Hara Kitsui, a Japanese boy.

At first they sold only coloured silks imported from the East, but within a year the other half of the shop had been taken and a whole range of goods from the Far and Near East was available. The architect, E.W. Godwin (1833–1886), who in 1884 was appointed to supervise Liberty's Costume Department, in an article published in *The Architect* (23 December 1876) described not only the distinguished crowd of customers but how the shop is 'from front to back and top to bottom literally crammed

Above: *Design for 'Freda' dress, a plate from* Dress and Decoration, *c. 1905*

with objects of oriental manufacture'. He went on to remark that: 'If it only had a little decent furniture, an artist might almost decorate and furnish his rooms from this one shop. There are matting and mats. carpets and rugs for the floor; Japanese papers for the walls; curtain stuffs for windows and doors; folding screens, chairs, stools and so forth.' He particularly admired the Japanese imports, albeit regretting that catering for the European market was already debasing Japanese art. He singled out for special praise:

... one inexpensive article, the little lacquer ash tray selling for sixpence, that bears the unmistakable imprint of that artistic Nation to which so many of us are directly or indirectly indebted. On one are a bit of weather-beaten bamboo and a butterfly; on another, one plant of the iris . . . ; on a third, a few naked branches; on a fourth, a baby bamboo shooting up like an arrow, each and all designed with a felicity and drawn with a freedom, and withal a delicacy, that is unmatchable by any other Nation!

Above: *A 'Liberty style' dining room, a watercolour, c. 1905*

There is little doubt that Liberty did a great deal to foster the 'cult of Japan', which was an integral part of the aesthetic movement in the 1870s and 1880s, but the shop also popularized a whole range of goods from other parts of the Far and Near East, what their advertisements described as 'Ancient and Modern Eastern Art Manufactures from Persia, India, China and Japan', together with embroideries, rugs, screens, tables and chairs from Morocco, Turkey and other parts of the Near East.

Arthur Liberty's success was such that by 1878 he was able to acquire two adjoining premises at 42 and 43 Kingly Street, with a wholesale section in Argyll Street. In 1883 further premises in Regent Street became vacant, which he named Chesham House in honour of his birthplace, enabling further expansion to take place, with an Eastern Bazaar in the basement, a Curio Department and an Arab Tearoom.

Not content with merely importing foreign goods, Arthur Liberty travelled abroad to see for himself, combining business with pleasure. In 1888–9, accompanied by the painter Sir Alfred East (1849–1913) and Charles Holme, a Bradford business man and Christopher Dresser's partner in Dresser and Holme, Mr and Mrs Liberty visited Japan. Before embarking on the trip, Arthur Liberty consulted Christopher Dresser, who had made an official visit to Japan in 1876–7. Dresser put him in touch with a number of his Japanese friends and associates. While in Japan, Arthur Liberty gave a lecture at the Tokyo National Museum on the 'Art Productions of Japan', dealing with the interrelation of influences between Japan and the West, stressing how the Japanese influence had permeated every European decorative art manufacture, particularly fabrics, pottery and printing. On his return, in 1890, he gave a similar lecture on 'The Industrial Arts and Manufactures of Japan' to the Society of Arts in London, a

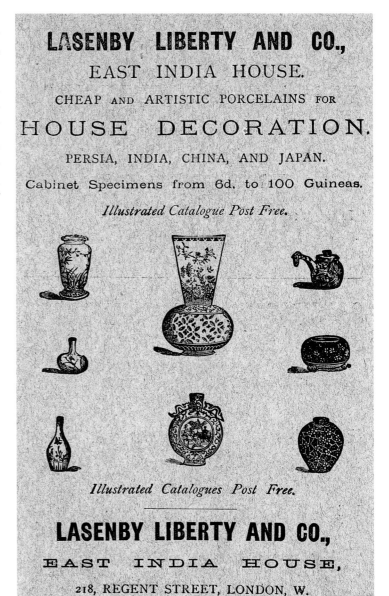

Above: *One of Liberty's very first advertisements, c. 1875*

Opposite above: *An advertisement for 'Liberty' Art Fabrics*

Opposite below: *Wallpaper frieze designed for Liberty's by Rex Silver*

FELICITOUS QUOTATIONS.

Hostess (of Upper Tooting, showing new house to Friend). "WE'RE VERY PROUD OF THIS ROOM, MRS. HOMINY. OUR OWN LITTLE
UPHOLSTERER DID IT UP JUST AS YOU SEE IT, AND ALL OUR FRIENDS THINK IT WAS *LIBERTY!*".
Visitor (sotto voce). "'OH, LIBERTY, LIBERTY, HOW MANY CRIMES ARE COMMITTED IN THY NAME!'"

lecture for which he was awarded a
Silver Medal. He also visited Tangier and
Istanbul, and in 1910 he and his wife
visited Granada, which must have re-
minded him of the Moorish schemes of
the early days of the firm.

Already by the 1890s Arthur Liberty
had become something of an establishment figure and one of the most re-
spected men of his generation; he was a
member of a number of learned soci-
eties including the Society of Arts, a
member of the Council of the London
Chamber of Commerce and Master of
the Glass Sellers Company. At the same

Above: *From* Punch, *20 October 1894*

Opposite: *Advertisement, from the back
of a Liberty's* Silks *catalogue*

time he began to live the life of a
country squire at The Lee Manor in
Buckinghamshire, four miles from his
birthplace at Chesham. During the few
years preceding the First World War,
he no longer travelled daily to London,
concentrating on his country duties as
High Sheriff of Buckinghamshire, a
Justice of the Peace, a County Council-

lor and Deputy Lieutenant of the County. It was for these services, rather than those of commerce, that he was knighted in 1913. He had no children and when he died on 11 May 1917, he made his nephew Ivor Stewart his heir, stipulating that he adopted the name of Stewart-Liberty.

The later expansion of Liberty's, including the new Tudor Building of 1924, need not concern us in dealing with the role of Arthur Liberty as a promoter of the aesthetic movement and a pioneer in making art nouveau, regarded by some as an unhealthy continental manifestation, acceptable to the British public.

His role in this was aptly summed up by Sir George Birdwood (1832–1917), the Anglo-Indian official and author, when he introduced a lecture on 'English Furniture' given by Arthur Lasenby Liberty at The Society of Arts on 13 March 1900 (*Society of Arts Journal*, vol. XLVIII, 1899–1900, p. 369 *et seq.*). Pointing out that Mr Lasenby Liberty's name was known all over the world in connection with furnishing and household decoration, he went on to say:

> . . . *the only point of interest in Mr Lasenby Liberty's commercial success for us is that it had been achieved on artistic lines. Mr Lasenby Liberty was one of the distinguished men of business in London who had identified themselves by natural instinct and reasoned conviction with the revival of industrial art during the Great Victorian era . . . his predominating purpose throughout having been to seek through simplifying — and that in cost as well as style — to beautify and dignify all the material accessories of our characteristic English home life.*

How he did this we shall see in the succeeding chapters, devoted separately to textiles, wallpapers and carpets; costume and embroideries; furniture; silver, metalwork and jewellery; and ceramics and glass, concentrating particularly on the work of the distinguished designers of these products.

A textile designed by Allan Vigers. Unnamed

14

Chapter One

TEXTILES, WALLPAPERS AND CARPETS

From the very first days, in 1875, the name Liberty has been more closely associated with textiles than any other product. The earliest fabrics were silks imported from the Near and Far East, but from the 1880s, Liberty began to commission designs from Christopher Dresser, Lindsay P. Butterfield, Walter Crane and other leading artists of the day. 'Liberty Art Fabrics' were to achieve worldwide renown and their influence in popularizing the art nouveau style was such that in Italy, for example, it became known as 'Stile Liberty'. The art nouveau style, with its sinuous, undulating lines, also predominated in Liberty's wallpapers and carpets.

From the foundation of the firm in 1875, the name of Liberty has been more closely associated with textiles than with any other form of merchandise. In June 1888 *The Journal of Decorative Art* devoted the fourth of their series on 'Famous Art Workers' to Liberty & Co., and stated that:

In no department of their enterprise have they been more successful than in that of their fabrics. Here they have achieved a veritable triumph, because their productions are accepted as the standards of colour taste, and a 'Liberty Fabric' is a password into the best of houses. Indeed, 'Liberty Colours' has become a synonym for soft, delicate shades, and they have the distinction shared with but few . . . of having their name passed into the current vernacular, as descriptive of certain qualities.

Above: *'Tanjore Lotus', an Indian inspired design*

The earliest of the Liberty silks imported from the East were recalled by William Judd in 1924 as 'the sort of thing that William Morris, Alma-Tadema and Burne-Jones and Rossetti used to come in and turn over and rave about'. Unfortunately, the native dyes were found to be fugitive and not always consistent in colour. To overcome this problem, Arthur Liberty turned to Thomas Wardle, the Leek silk printer and dyer who was already printing textiles for William Morris, and with whom he had carried out numerous experiments with vegetable dyes.

He was successful in producing a wide range of artistic and aesthetic colours from 'the faintest amber to the deepest sunset gold, the palest cerulean blue to the darkest sapphire, the daintiest rose-blush to the richest maple red' and 'Persian Pink, Venetian Red, Terracotta, Ochre-Yellow, Sapphire and Peacock Blue, Sage, Olive, Willow Green, Soft Brown and Drab'.

A series of Liberty fabrics, woven in India, but dyed and printed at Leek, were shown by Thomas Wardle in the British India Pavilion at the Paris Universal Exhibition of 1878, where they were purchased for the Animal Products Division of the South Kensington Museum (now the Victoria & Albert Museum). Printed on tussore and mysore silk, in non-fugitive colours, the designs were of Eastern inspiration and were given Indian sounding names — Mooltan May-Blossom, Rangoon Poppy, Tanjore Lotus, Chamba Chrysanthemum, Oodypoor, Salangore and Allahabad Marigold — the latter also printed in gold as a cheaper substitute for a woven silk and gold brocade. They received enthusiastic press reports: *The Mayfair*, using aesthetic terminology, wrote 'These soft silks are all 'sincere', while *The Medical Examiner* could 'imagine nothing more delightful', and even *La Mode Illustrée* recognized competition in describing them as 'The best finished silks we have seen'. Comment from more scholarly quarters, from Sir Phillip Cunliffe Owen, Director of the South Kensington Museum, and Dr (later Sir George) Birdwood, of the India Office, was equally enthusiastic. Dr Birdwood particularly admired those that were exact reproductions from wood-blocks in the India Museum

Below: Page from Liberty's Silks catalogue, c. 1895. Drawing by J. Moyr Smith

ORIENTAL SILKS woven exclusively for LIBERTY & CO. Ltd.

"Liberty" Silks.

Hand-Block-Printed, in Varied Designs and colourings.
Dyed and Printed in England.   Woven in India.

THE PRINTED "LIBERTY" SILKS are woven in India, and imported in what is technically termed the "grey" state.

IN THE GREY STATE the Silks are Dyed (in England) and Printed by a special Hand-process, in which the latest Chemical and Scientific Knowledge is utilized to ensure the Stability of the Colouring Pigments applied.

THE CHARACTERISTIC AND BEAUTIFUL DESIGNS are the result of careful study and selection extending over a long series of years.

CONTEMPORARY DECORATIVE ARTISTS of acknowledged repute have been employed in the production of many of the Designs.

AMONG THE DESIGNS may be found reproductions of Ancient Indian, Persian, and other Classic Oriental Originals.   34 inches wide.

Price **28/6** per Piece of about 7 Yards.

Half-pieces cut without extra charge.

PATTERNS POST FREE.

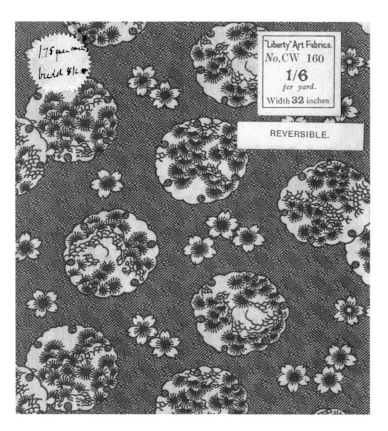

Left: '*Mooltan*', *a reversible printed cotton furnishing fabric, c. 1880*

Right: *Reversible printed cotton, designed by Christopher Dresser for Liberty's, 1882*

which *The Artist* of April 1881 considered 'a good thought, giving as it does to their beautiful goods a stamp of artistic sensibility'.

The fabrics were either exact copies or adaptations of Indian and Persian designs, but about two years later Liberty began to commission original designs from leading professional designers. One of the first to be approached by Arthur Liberty was Dr Christopher Dresser, who was to become a close friend and whom he had probably met for the first time in 1878.

Christopher Dresser

Dresser, an exact contemporary of William Morris, was born in Glasgow in 1834, and entered the Government School of Design at Marlborough House at the age of 13, where he showed an exceptional talent for botanical illustration and an enthusiasm for Oriental art, particularly Japanese. While still a student he won a prize for 'Garment Fabrics' which were printed on cambric by the firm of Liddiard & Co. – for Hargreaves Brothers & Co. – and he was later to become not only a designer of textiles but the leading industrial designer of his day, and the most prominent exponent of the 'cult of Japan', which country he visited as an official guest in 1876–77. His daughter Nellie, in a letter to the Victoria & Albert Museum in 1952, recalled that Dresser supplied a number of textile designs to Liberty's in 1882. Only one of these has been positively identified, a design with a dragon on a fretted ground (now in the Nordiska Museum, Stockholm), but some of the printed cotton furniture fabrics illustrated in a Liberty catalogue of about 1882 may be from his hand. One in particular, although given the Indian sounding name of 'Mooltan', has a typical Japanese design of irregular circular motifs filled with flowers, ferns and pine fronds on a fretted ground scattered with blossom. It corresponds closely to some of his designs for Minton's, and three other designs entitled 'Juggernaut', 'Pooree' and 'Dhama' may well be by him. Apart from textiles, metalwork and glass designed by Dresser were sold by Liberty's, and his son Louis joined their staff after his return from Japan where he had managed the Kobe branch of his father's company, Dresser & Holme, which had been set up in 1878 for the importation of Japanese goods into Britain.

J. Moyr Smith, who had trained as a designer in Dresser's studio, in his book *Ornamental Interiors Ancient and Modern* (London, 1887) praised the Liberty fabrics as having 'done not a little to render artistic decoration a matter of comparative ease . . . Many of the silks are printed with Indian designs of graceful patterns . . . these are especially well adapted for wall decoration as well as for curtains'. One such Indian printed silk in shades of terracotta was used in the drawing room at Rutland Cottage, belonging to the Earl of Cadogan, and Moyr Smith used one printed in gold on a pale greenish yellow ground in a scheme for a drawing room.

Liberty's designated their textiles as 'Art Fabrics', 'art' being the fashionable term to distinguish goods which

Below: *A sample book of Madras muslins dating from the 1890s*

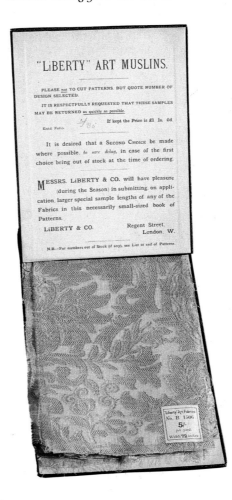

Above: *Two Silver Studio designs produced for Liberty's by Arthur Silver in 1896. The left one is printed velveteen, the right one is printed cotton*

were considered superior to the normal run of ordinary commercial manufacture; hence 'art fabrics' joined the already established terms of 'art furniture' and 'art pottery'. Samples of these fabrics bore a paper label printed with 'LIBERTY ART FABRICS', a serial number, the width, price per yard, and sometimes in addition their registered 'Lotus' trademark.

A catalogue of **Liberty Art Fabrics**, issued in October 1883, stated that:

Messrs. Liberty & Co. have made it their special study to reproduce — with due regard to the requirements of Modern times — the beautiful soft-clinging Draperies so much esteemed in ancient Greece . . . cotton, silk and wool are used separately and individually but 'shoddy' materials are utterly rejected. Silk is called silk, and cotton cotton, and will be found in each instance to justify its name.

Following the earlier success at the Paris Exhibition of 1878, Liberty Art Fabrics were awarded a Gold Medal at

Above: *A printed cotton by Arthur Silver, 1896. A similar design appears in* Art & Decoration, *1897*

Overleaf left: *Jacquard woven wool doublecloth by C.F.A. Voysey*

Overleaf right: *Block printed cushion cover, designed by Silver Studio. 1904*

Amsterdam in 1883, and those intended specifically for dress were awarded a Silver Medal at the Rational Dress Exhibition of 1883. Moyr Smith was responsible for some of the illustrations in the Liberty catalogues of the 1880s and 1890s, including the typically 'aesthetic' ladies in 'mediaeval' dress which embellished their *Silks* catalogue.

As well as using Thomas Wardle to print their fabrics, Liberty's also used Littler's print works at Merton Abbey from the late 1870s, print works which they actually acquired in 1904. However, from the beginning, most of their fabrics were produced by contract printers and weavers, both at home and abroad, and it is extremely difficult to discern the exact provenance of some of the fabrics. In some cases Liberty's would commission a design from an artist or design studio directly, while in others a textile manufacturer would sell a finished product to Liberty's, to be sold exclusively by them.

The closest association of Liberty's with a design studio was that with the Silver Studio, set up in 1880 by Arthur Silver, an association that continued until the closure of the studio in 1965. Arthur Silver (1853–1896), after attending Reading School of Art was apprenticed to the designer H.W. Batley, who was much influenced by Japanese art. In 1880 Arthur Silver founded the Silver Studio at Hammersmith, and began to supply designs to many manufacturers. He also launched the 'Silvern Series' of photographs of historic textiles, drawn from the collections of the Victoria & Albert Museum, which he sold as basic source material to a number of firms, including Liberty's, who used them for some of their wallpaper designs.

His 'Peacock Feather' design, roller-printed by the Rossendale Printing Co.,

shown at the Manchester Royal Jubilee Exhibition in 1887 and later renamed the 'Hera', was revived for Liberty's Centenary in 1975 and has remained a best-seller ever since. Peacock feathers were one of the main motifs of the aesthetic movement, but most of Arthur Silver's designs in the 1890s are best described as art nouveau, characterized by swirling designs of waves, trees and sprays of flowers with undulating stalks, tulips and Glasgow-style roses, often with a discrepancy of scale between the various elements. Not only Arthur Silver, but a number of other artists employed by the

Above: 'Peacock feather', printed cotton, designed by Arthur Silver

Silver Studios also designed for Liberty's, including John Illingworth Kay (1870–1950) and Harry Napper (1860–1940), both of whose designs were also strongly art nouveau. Another important designer associated with the Silver Studio was Archibald Knox (1864–1933) who produced textile and rug designs, often with Celtic motifs, but is now best known for his designs for Liberty silver and pewter.

Many prominent designers

John Illingworth Kay worked for the Silver Studio from about 1892 to 1900, producing designs for book covers, wallpapers and textiles. During this period, he probably also worked freelance and in 1900 left the Studio to manage the stencilling department of the wallpaper firm of Essex & Co. He was also a talented watercolour painter, and in 1922 left Essex & Co. to take up a part-time teaching post at the Central School of Arts and Crafts.

Like John Illingworth Kay, Harry Napper was another prominent watercolour artist, and as well as designing textiles, he also designed furniture, metalwork and wallpaper. He joined the Silver Studio in about 1893, and after Arthur Silver's death in 1896, managed the studio's design production for two years, leaving in 1898 to work on a freelance basis, but continuing to sell designs through the Silver Studio. His designs are more stylized than those of the other members, and sometimes border on the eccentric, appealing to continental as well as English tastes, a number of his designs being sold to French manufacturers as well as to Liberty, and other British firms.

Even closer to continental art nouveau were the designs of Léon Victor Solon (1872–1957), the son of the ceramist Marc Louis Emanuel Solon (1835–1913), who was employed at Sèvres from 1857, where he specialized in *pâte-sur-pâte* decoration, a process he brought to Minton's in 1870. Like his father, Léon Victor Solon worked for Minton's from 1900–1909, but he also designed posters and textiles in the 1890s. One of his most striking designs, an allegorical design with kneeling figures, naked boys and classical masks interspersed in a network of gnarled and knotted branches, was printed on velveteen for Liberty's by Thomas Wardle in 1892. This textile was later illustrated in the *Studio* (vol. III, 1894, p. 95) and he also designed posters for the *Studio*. At Minton, together with John Wadsworth he introduced their 'Secessionist' ware in 1902 and also tube-lined tiles with figure subjects, all in a rather continental art nouveau style. In 1909 he emigrated to the United States, where he was responsible for the decoration of the Philadelphia Museum of Art.

John Llewellyn

Much of the credit for the 'Art Fabrics' of the 1890s must go to John Llewellyn, who joined the Silk Department of Libertys in 1889, having worked for Howell & James, a shop closely associated with the aesthetic movement. In 1891 John Llewellyn was put in charge of the Silk Department, and in 1898 became a director. He was responsible for the commissioning and purchase of designs, and for liaison with the contract printers and weavers. He had excellent taste and a real enthusiasm for textiles, as well as an instinct for picking the best designers. An article in *The Citizen* of Saturday, 10 December 1898 entitled BRITISH INDUSTRIES. *Pioneers of Commerce, No. 24.* LIBERTY & CO., LIMITED, after a brief description of the foundation of the firm, was devoted mainly to textiles and an interview with John Llewellyn and John W. Howe, one of the two managing directors. The writer described how:

. . . the latest patterns were spread out before me one after the other, and really they were all so excellent and so fascinating that it would have been difficult to make a selection, but a silk tapestry, in four different colourings, at 8/9p a yard, 50 inches wide, which I was assured could not have been purchased ten years ago under guineas a yard, specially attracted attention.

Unfortunately, it has not been possible to identify this particular fabric, but as John Llewellyn explained to the reporter:

These and other and similar characteristic patterns are now all the rage, not only in England, but on the Continent, and, indeed, throughout the World, just in the same way as there was a Louis XVI period, so we flatter ourselves that we have created a new 'English' period. Years ago nothing but French designs would suit, now the English School is leading. Mr Howe, when asked, 'Where do you get your designs from?' replied, 'It is no matter to us where a design comes from so long as it possesses merits worthy to be put before the public by the House of Liberty. We collect designs from all quarters, and our manufacturing friends are only too pleased for us to suggest the designs which should be taken up.'

This approach provided a wide variety of designs while maintaining a distinct 'house style'.

C.F.A. Voysey

The architect C.F.A. Voysey (1857–1941), one of the most original and influential designers of his generation, was to produce many designs for Liberty's from the late 1880s onwards, and although he professed to abhor the style, his work did much to promote art nouveau, particularly on the Continent. Among Voysey's designs for Liberty's, both printed by G.P. and J. Baker, was one of scrolling flowers and leaves with crested birds, dating from 1893, and one with stylized birds and tulips. Alexander Morton & Co. produced many of his woven fabrics for Liberty, including a silk and wool double-cloth with a strange design of stags and swans with stylized trees and a flight of birds above. This and 'The Strawberry' were used as upholstery fabrics. Voysey also designed carpets for Liberty's, both for the hand-knotted Donegal range and the machine woven carpets made by Tomkinson and Adam.

Charles Francis Annesley Voysey, the eldest son of a rather unorthodox clergyman, was born near Hull. In 1871 the family moved to London, and in 1874 at the age of 17, Voysey was apprenticed to the Gothic Revival architect, J.P. Seddon. Four years later, in 1882, he set up in practice on his

Opposite: *A roller printed cotton made for Liberty's in 1894. Designer unknown*

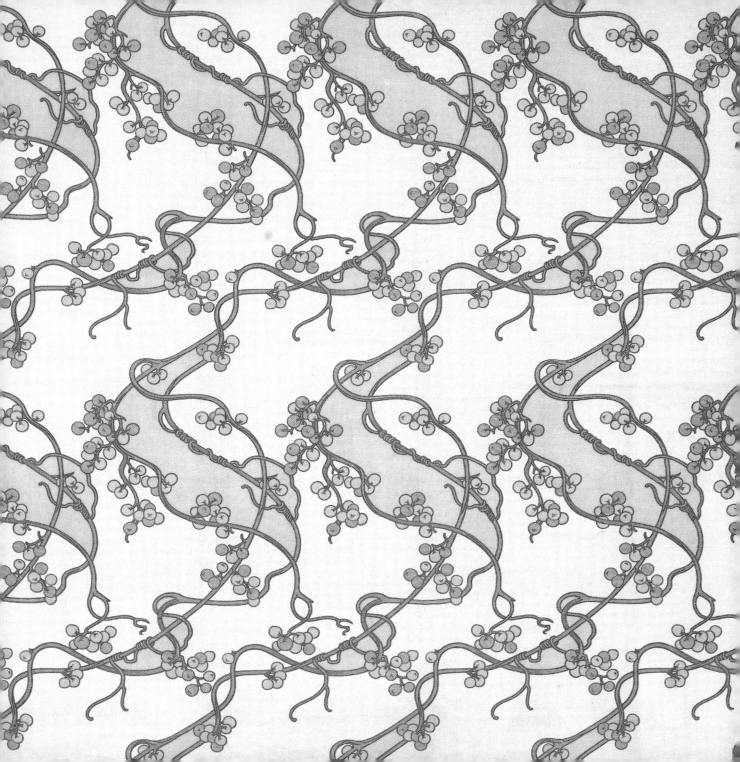

Above: 'The Agra', an Indian inspired fabric designed by Lewis F. Day

Opposite: 'The Four Seasons', a Walter Crane design on printed velveteen. 1892

flat pattern design continued to form a major part of his output. His earliest designs show the influence of William Morris with traditional repeats based on historical forms, but by the mid 1890s his work was characterized by flowing patterns combining birds, animals, hearts, trees, leaves and flowers, treated in silhouette.

Another leading designer of flat pattern whose fabrics were sold by Liberty's was Lewis F. Day (1845–1910). The son of a Quaker wine merchant, he was born in London and began his artistic career in 1864 in the office of the stained glass manufacturers, Lavers and Barraud, and later with Clayton and Bell. In 1870 he worked with Heaton, Butler and Bayne on the decoration of Eaton Hall, at the same time as starting his own business designing stained glass, tiles, wallpapers and textiles for many manufacturers, including Turnbull and Stockdale, whose Art Director he became in 1881. He was a founder member of the Art Workers' Guild in 1884 and later the Master, and in 1888 a member of the Arts and Crafts Exhibition Society. He was also a frequent contributor to the art periodicals of the day and a prolific writer of books on all aspects of ornament and design, books that were to run to numerous editions and influence several generations of art students. His own designs, based on an extensive knowledge of historic ornament combined with natural and Japanese elements, although commercially successful, lack the freshness and originality found in the work of many of his contemporaries.

own. Finding it difficult to obtain commissions, on the advice of his friend A.H. Mackmurdo (the founder of the Century Guild), in 1883 he began to design wallpapers and textiles. Although he was later to achieve success as an architect and furniture designer,

Walter Crane

Equally prominent as a writer on ornament and design was Walter Crane (1845–1915), the son of an artist, who was born in Liverpool. In 1859 he was apprenticed to a radical London wood engraver, William Linton, and soon progressed to book illustration, first in black and white, and then to colour wood-block illustration for children's books. Like Godwin, he was an early admirer of Japanese art, but he was eclectic in his sources, drawing on the whole repertoire of historic ornament. He produced designs for most of the decorative arts including stained glass, mosaics, tiles and ceramics, textiles, embroidery and tapestry, but his greatest skill was in designing wallpapers, producing over fifty designs for Jeffrey & Co., from 1874 onwards. He was a founder member of the Art Workers' Guild, serving as Master from 1888–9, and President of the Arts and Crafts Exhibition Society, founded in 1888. In 1893 he was appointed Director of Design at Manchester School of Art, and in 1898 was for one year Principal of the Royal College of Art. His work was much admired abroad, both in Europe and the United States, being shown at Bing's Maison de l'Art Nouveau in Paris, with Les Vingt in Brussels, with the Secessionists in Vienna, and in major exhibitions abroad, including the Philadelphia Centennial Exhibition of 1876 and the Turin Exhibition of 1902.

Walter Crane designed at least one textile that was sold by Liberty's. This was the 'Four Seasons', an allegorical design of classically draped females,

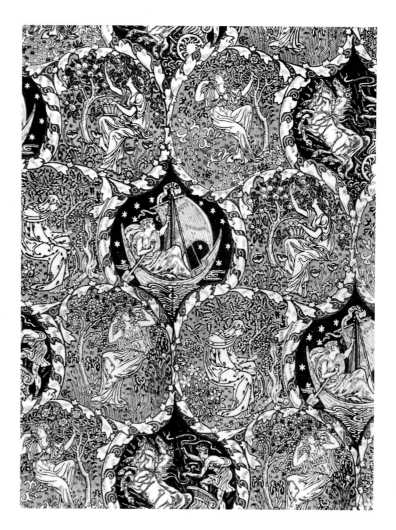

with Apollo in his chariot and a figure representing the moon surrounded by stars. It was printed by Wardle on both tussore silk and velveteen, and shown at the Arts and Crafts Exhibition of 1893.

Walter Crane used a Liberty fabric in the dining room of his house in Holland Street, Kensington. This was a design of alternating horizontal rows of daffodils and crocuses designed by Arthur Willcock, a prolific freelance designer, whose work featured in an article in *The Artist* in 1900.

One of the most talented freelance designers of Liberty fabrics was Lindsay P. Butterfield (1869–1948), who combined the influences of both William Morris and C.F.A. Voysey to produce designs that were entirely his own. He left school at 18 and worked in a West Indian merchant's office from 1887–8, while attending evening classes at the Lambeth School of Art, and completed his training at the National Art Training School at South Kensington, where he won a number of prizes. By 1894 he had established himself as a first-class designer of both textiles and wallpapers. He specialized in floral designs, often with poppies or daffodils, treated in a restrained art nouveau style, which were printed on cotton and velveteen, or woven as silk and wool double-cloths by Alexander Morton & Co. One of them, a rather Japanese design of iris and berries of about 1896, was included in the Liberty Art Fabrics range as 'The Lomond', and sold for 6s 6d a yard. Another silk with a design of poppies and leaves, called 'The Iveagh', was woven by Warners in 1901. Three Liberty cretonnes by Butterfield, the 'Aloe', 'Potentilla' and 'Tutson', were illustrated in the *Art Journal* of 1901 (p. 369 *et seq.*). Butterfield also taught at the Kingston and Camberwell Art Schools and in 1909 was instrumental in forming the Design Club, which had premises in Newman Street, with the aim of furthering good design by bringing together designers and manufacturers in one organization. One of those on the manufacturing side was Arthur Lasenby Liberty. From 1905 Lindsay Butterfield taught textile design at the Victoria & Albert Museum to recipients of the P.A.B. Widener Fellowship awarded by the Philadelphia School of Design for Women. In 1926 Butterfield sold two of the designs of one of his American students, Alice Dorothy Few, to Liberty which they marketed as the 'Bird and Wisteria' and 'Chinese Panel' cretonnes.

A number of Lindsay Butterfield's designs were revived in 1960, along with others by Harry Napper and J. Scarrett Rigby. They were printed as dress fabrics on silk, wool and cotton, and named 'The Lotus' range after Liberty's original trademark, a collection that was used by the great couturiers of London, Paris and Rome.

John Scarrett Rigby, whose work featured in the 1960 revival, was designing textiles by 1889. He produced printed fabrics for G.P. and J. Baker and woven fabrics for Alexander Morton & Co. which were sold through Liberty's, and was a founder member of The Society of Designers. His designs frequently feature rather ragged poppies, sometimes with huge acanthus leaves, and have the typical swirling motions of art nouveau.

Another specialist in floral design, whose work was sold by Liberty's, was

Above: 'The Hydrangea', one of Lindsay Butterfield's floral designs

Below: 'The Lomond' by Lindsay Butterfield, printed on silk and wool doublecloth

Allan Francis Vigers (1858–1921). Trained as an architect, he specialized also in illumination, but he is best known for minutely detailed floral patterns for textiles and wallpapers drawn with almost botanical accuracy, often on a white ground, which set off his fresh, clear colours. Alternatively, he favoured a blue ground, giving a deeper, richer effect. He exhibited at the Arts and Crafts Exhibitions of 1896, 1903, and 1916, and his work was frequently illustrated in the *Studio*.

Other designers whose textiles were sold by Liberty's in the 1890s and early 1900s were Arthur Willshaw and Edgar L. Pattison. Little is known about Arthur Willshaw, who was active from about 1875, and designed silk and wool woven textiles, mostly produced by J.W. & C. Ward of Halifax, which were sold through Liberty's. These are illustrated in the *Artist* (May to August, 1899, pp. 17–21). Most of the designs are floral, in a flowing art nouveau style, but they include an Empire style curtain and a bordered and fringed table cloth with a rose motif. Edgar L. Pattison, who was active from about 1896, was a decorative painter and a designer of furniture, wallpapers, textiles, costume and embroidery. His designs tend to be more traditional and formalized.

'Stile Liberty'

Many of these Liberty textiles were illustrated in the art periodicals of the time, including foreign periodicals such

Below: *A roller printed cotton, printed for Liberty's, c. 1895–1900*

as *Art et Décoration* and *Der Moderne Stil*, but the name of the designer is rarely given, and many of them remain unattributed. Known throughout the world, these Liberty 'Art Fabrics' of the 1890s which bore their 'Lotus' trademark, had a phenomenal success and one result was that in Italy the art nouveau style was christened 'Stile Liberty'. The fabrics were sold not only by Liberty's own retail outlets in Regent Street, in the provinces, and in Paris, but also by agents throughout Europe, including Samuel Bing's Maison de l'Art Nouveau in Paris, Burchard Söhne, Berlin, and Braes in Düsseldorf. Many European museums have fine collections of Liberty textiles bought at the time of production. Liberty's also had agents in New York, Boston, Chicago, Toronto and Tasmania, and even in Shanghai and Japan.

The art nouveau style reached its peak about 1900; although it lingered on for the first decade of the 20th century it had lost its original impetus, and the designs tended to be simpler and more formal and often on a smaller scale, more suited to the oak 'cottage' type furniture. Along with other manufacturers Liberty began to cater for more conservative tastes, with typical Edwardian chintzes with roses, and ribbons, warp-printed cretonnes, and woven fabrics based on Spanish or Portuguese designs or traditional English damasks. Some good original designs continued to be produced, including 'The Chats-

Below: *'The Milford', one of Liberty's more formal designs dating from the early 1900s*

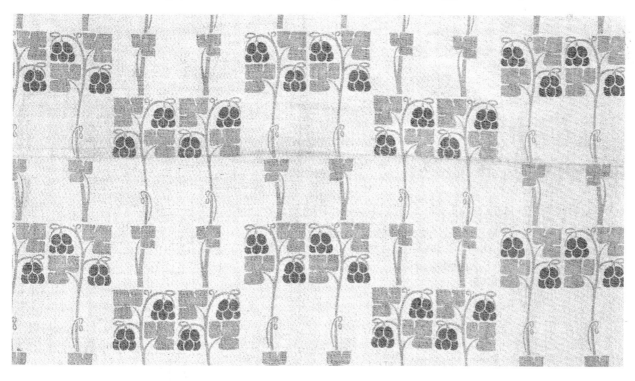

33

worth', a design of fruit trees, and 'The Lowther', a design of flowers and buds, which were registered in December 1909. Both were designed by Sidney Mawson (d. 1941), a landscape artist and prolific designer of textiles and wallpapers, who was much influenced by William Morris. One of the interesting Liberty innovations during the first decade of the 20th century was boldly printed cotton cushion covers for nursery use; some were designed by the Silver Studio, others by William Kidd, who also designed nursery wallpaper friezes for Liberty's. One of his cushion designs shows Dutch children at play. Children and adults in traditional Dutch costume were a very popular subject about 1905 appearing on tiles, ceramics and biscuit tins as well as on textiles and wallpapers.

Wallpapers

In 1875, when Liberty's was founded, wall surfaces were normally divided into three horizontal sections of dado, filling and frieze, and decorated to differentiate the three sections. The dado, which reached from the skirting to a rail about 106.7cm (3ft 6in) from the floor, was usually the darkest in tone, although the avant-garde may have followed E.W. Godwin in covering this with straw matting, which they could have bought from Liberty's. The filling would normally be a patterned wallpaper, and the frieze, above the picture rail, might be a specially designed matching frieze, or moulded plaster, or as in the home of Linley Sambourne, the cartoonist, at 18, Stafford Terrace in Kensington, two different wallpapers might serve as filling and frieze.

The earliest wallpapers sold by Liberty's were imported Japanese embossed papers, made to simulate leather. In his article in *The Architect* (23 December 1876), Godwin praised one particular wallpaper, a broad pattern of dark green meandering foliage on a gold ground, which he felt 'would of itself give a style to a house that had none'. Others, he felt, were only suitable for filling up small panels of cheap furniture – no doubt some of the cheaper varieties of

Below: *A Japanese leather wallpaper imported by Liberty's, c. 1890*

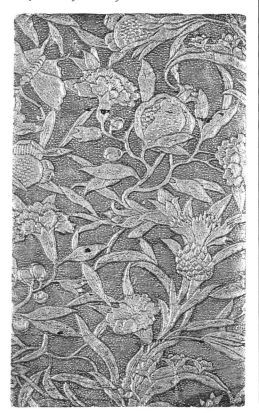

Anglo-Japanese bamboo furniture. These Japanese leather papers were popular for reception rooms. A typical example, embossed with a gold floral design on a red ground, and possibly bought from Liberty's, was used by Linley Sambourne in his drawing room. They were used not only for the filling but also for dadoes.

In 1887 a Paper-Hanging Department was set up in Chesham House, and William Judd, who had been Arthur Lasenby Liberty's assistant at Farmer & Rogers, was put in charge. A range of single colour designs called the 'Damasque Wallpapers', designed by a Mr Fletcher, was introduced. Wallpapers from various manufacturers were added, no doubt including some designed by the Silver Studio, and Liberty's began to issue their own wallpaper books.

Little is known about the Liberty wallpapers of the late 1880s and early 1890s, but the *Handbook of Sketches, Part II*, dating from after 1893, devotes a page to wallpapers, unfortunately unillustrated, but mentioning their 'Damasque Wallpapers' to which many new, exclusive and registered designs have been added. In decorative effect they resemble 'Rich Silken Brocades'. The advertisement also drew attention to their Japanese leather papers including many of exclusive design, and also fine reproductions of Old Venetian and Spanish models.

A photograph by Bedford Lemere of a Liberty bedroom of 1897 shows an elaborate floral wallpaper, typical of the art nouveau designs of the Silver Studio,

Above: *'The Richmond' stencilled wallpaper frieze, Silver Studio, c. 1895*

Overleaf left: *An original design for wallpaper by Silver Studio, 1899*

Overleaf right: *A wallpaper frieze designed by Silver Studio and printed by Shand Kydd, 1895*

with a broad, similar style frieze above. An illustration of the 'Helga' bedroom suite in the 1902 *Furniture* catalogue shows a Voysey wallpaper, and his wallpapers, like his textiles, were no doubt sold by Liberty's.

As Aymer Vallance wrote in the *Magazine of Art* in 1898 (pp. 501–502) 'Not very many years ago, the dado was the essential feature in an artistically decorated room. Today, fashion or better taste has pronounced in favour of the frieze instead'. Liberty's certainly followed this trend, and most of the Liberty interiors around the turn of the century show a broad frieze, sometimes as deep as 90cm (3ft), with a plain coloured wall below, sometimes of stretched linen or canvas. These friezes were often of stencilled wallpaper or canvas, with bold art nouveau floral designs in shaded colours, stylized peacocks (as with the 'Athelstan' suite), heart-shaped motifs and vine patterns with squared-up leaves. Several variations of trees with flights of birds, recalling the designs of Voysey and Knox, are also found, while others are in a typical 'Glasgow' style. The so-called 'Glasgow style' developed in the 1890s and centred around the Glasgow School of Art. The original exponents of the style were trained there, or had some connection with the School. The main motifs were organic, but highly stylized, with roses, foliage, butterflies and birds, attenuated human forms, and sinuous curves contrasting with taut, straight lines. Muted, somewhat off-beat colours were preferred, especially purple, lavender, pink, olive and milky greens. The influence of the Glasgow style was felt not only in Britain, but throughout Europe. Many examples are illustrated in the 1906 *Studio Year Book of Decorative Art*.

The Liberty Bazaar, described as 'A Permanent Exhibition of the most Characteristic Decorative Objects and Artist Manufactures of Europe and the Far East', published in 1898, devoted a section to nursery wallpapers:

Messrs. Liberty have a new series of wallpapers, designed by Cecil Aldin and John Hassall, specially for nursery use. The object is to place before children such pictures as are well drawn and well coloured, and thus train the eye in infancy to discriminate and enjoy artistic work. The present series consists of bold and simple Outline Pictures illustrating Nursery Rhymes, Domestic and Farmyard Animals, etc. These panels when framed also form excellent subjects for Nursery Pictures.

Above: *A wallpaper design by Harry Silver dating from the early 1900s*

Opposite: *A stylized design of trees and birds by the Silver Studio*

Illustrated were two upright panels 'Morning', with a child waking up in bed, and 'Night', showing a child saying her prayers. These were by John Hassall (1868–1948), a well-known book illustrator and poster artist. Two horizontal panels, 'Mother Duck' and 'Dog and Cock' were by Cecil Aldin, an artist famous for not only pictures of dogs and animals, but also hunting scenes. Other panels and friezes not necessarily confined to nursery use included landscape designs, Dutch scenes being especially popular. A typical example, 'The Dutch Landscape', a stencilled frieze which shows a tree lined road with cottages and a windmill, is illustrated in the 1906 *Studio Year Book of Decorative Art*, (p. 114). Many of these designs were probably executed by the Silver Studio, stencilled friezes being one of the Studio's specialities.

Carpets

From the beginning, Liberty's sold considerable quantities of carpets and rugs from Persia, Turkey, the Caucasus, India and China. *The Journal of Decorative Art* devoted the fourth of its series on *Famous Art Workers* to Liberty & Co. (June 1888, p. 87 *et seq.*) and gives a vivid description of their showrooms:

Stepping out of busy Regent Street into Messrs. Liberty's showrooms is as startling a transformation as any ever seen behind the footlights. The noise and glare of a London Street is suddenly exchanged for the stillness and the subdued tones of the Orient. Rich rugs lie under our feet, full toned but harmonious colours greet the eye from wall and roof and floor . . . Rooms hung with Oriental carpets and Eastern rugs . . . Messrs. Liberty have brought away the colour and taste of the lands of the Orient.

About this time, European carpets were added to their stock, but more importantly, about 1902, the firm began to commission hand-knotted Donegal carpets which were woven in Ireland under the direction of Alexander Morton & Co. Like Liberty's English silk venture, (page 48) this enterprise also had a philanthropic purpose, for it was undertaken in collaboration with the Irish Congested Districts Board to provide badly needed employment for female labour. Most of the carpets were in the art nouveau style, including designs by C.F.A. Voysey, but traditional Eastern patterns and conventional floral designs were included for more conservative tastes. In 1903 these Donegal carpets were promoted at an exhibition at the Grafton Galleries, which prompted the *Furniture Record* (vol. VIII, 1903, p. 251) to remark that the carpets 'have marked and distinctive characteristics in design and colouring, which will probably lead to making the carpet the starting point of the decorative scheme of a room, rather than the wallpaper as heretofore'. The carpets were also illustrated in the *Studio* (vol. XXVIII, 1903) and in the following year Liberty's mounted an exhibition of 'Modern Celtic Art', which had become their speciality, with a number of carpets and rugs with Celtic interlaced ornaments designed by Archibald Knox and Mrs G.F. Watts, the second wife of the painter. She must have been a formidable lady, for contrary to Liberty's normal practice, she was acknowledged as the designer of several exhibits.

The Donegal rugs and carpets fea-

Above: *'The Kinsale' hand-knotted Donegal carpet, c. 1903*

Opposite: *Hand-tufted Donegal rug made by Alexander Morton & Co. Possibly designed by Knox*

tured prominently in the 1906 *Studio Year Book of Decorative Art*. These included a fine interlaced Celtic design by Archibald Knox, a number of designs with Glasgow-style roses and a stylized vine design with bunches of grapes and leaves. In 1907 similar designs were shown in Liberty's premises in an exhibition of 'New Irish Hand-Made Carpets', accompanied by a catalogue explaining both the social and artistic aims of this Irish venture.

*Dress of striped Indian washing silk, designed by
Hamo Thorneycroft for his wife, c. 1881*

Chapter Two

COSTUME AND EMBROIDERIES

Liberty & Co. played a leading role in the dress reform movement of the late 19th century. The Costume Department was opened in 1884 and the soft, draping Liberty silks, velvets and cashmeres were made up into flowing 'aesthetic' styles, often inspired by historic originals. Embroidery enjoyed a revival at this time and Liberty's imported antique embroideries from Europe, Japan, China and the Near East. They also supplied silks and original designs for home embroideresses, both for furnishing and dress, and private lessons in embroidery techniques could be arranged by appointment.

The reform of fashionable dress, particularly for women and children, for health as well as for artistic reasons, was an important aspect of the aesthetic movement. The boned corsets and tight lacing were thought to displace the internal organs and distort posture, while the heavy fabrics, with voluminous skirts, impeded movement for women who were beginning to enter the professions and generally embark on a more active life. Liberty's were to play an important part in dress reform, not only by providing lighter fabrics, which draped more gracefully, but by setting up a Costume Department, with a studio and workrooms where dresses were designed and made up in Liberty fabrics. This department opened in 1884 and the architect, E.W. Godwin (1833–1886), was appointed as supervisor, at a fee of one guinea per hour for each hour's attendance at the studio. Godwin had already made a study of historic costume, was Hon. Secretary of the Costume Society, and lectured on 'Dress and its Relation to Health and Climate' at the International Health Exhibition, held at the Albert Hall in 1884. The appointment of an eminent architect obviously gave a certain cachet to the Liberty Costume Department, although the appointment was of brief duration as Godwin died in 1886.

A number of the designs were loosely based on historic costume, and often designated as 'Greek' or 'Medieval'. The typical 'aesthetic' dress was softly gathered and held at a high waist with a belt or sash, with a square or round neck edged with a white frill, and sleeves that

Above: *Dress of Liberty crepe with tunic of Liberty velvet. By Forma of London, 1912*

44

were puffed at the top but tight from just above the elbow. They were made in the Liberty silks, sometimes with a velvet overdress or surcoat, or in the Liberty 'Umritza' cashmere. This fabric, woven in England from East Indian wools in a wide range of colours, was cheaper and more durable than the Eastern product. Subsequently known purely as 'Liberty' cashmere, it was used for autumn and winter dresses and cloaks, while a thinner variety was considered suitable for summer wear and for children's dresses.

Smocking

Embroidery and smocking were often used as decoration. Smocking appears on the bodice of a dress of Liberty striped Indian washing silk, with puff sleeves, a square neck and a looped up overskirt, which is now in the Victoria & Albert Museum. This was designed about 1881 by the sculptor Hamo Thorneycroft for his wife. The Thorneycrofts were founder members of the Healthy and Artistic Dress Union in 1890 which launched a journal called *Aglaia* in 1893. It features designs for reformed dress for men, women and children by the artist Henry Holiday and by Walter Crane. Lasenby Liberty wrote an article 'on the progress of taste in dress' for *Aglaia* in 1894, and a number of the designs in the Liberty catalogue of the 1890s parallel the designs by Walter Crane.

The Lady's World, a periodical edited by Mrs Oscar Wilde, featured two Liberty tea gowns in the July issue of 1887 (pp. 291–2). The text described these silk tea gowns as being 'usually made as long flowing robes with inserted fronts of contrasting colour, draped from neck to foot with a frilling of gauze, crepe de chine or soft fine silk close up into the throat'. Another was made of the Umritza cashmere with Turkish embroidery edging the fronts, which fell in straight lines from the shoulder over a 'loose front of pale green Nagpore'. The same issue of *The Lady's World* illustrates the 'Mab Smock', as worn by the actress Mabel Millet, made of light blue cashmere and embroidered and smocked in silk. Girl's Lawn Tennis Dresses by Liberty, similarly smocked, were also illustrated – not surprisingly, as Mrs Oscar Wilde was much concerned with the revival of the country craft of smocking. *The Woman's World* (vol. III, 1890, p. 223) describes how 'when the fashionable revival of this difficult craft began . . . the artistic modistes had to send their delicate ''Liberty'' silks down to humble cottages in this county [Sussex] and in Dorsetshire where a few conservative rustics still adhere to the old smock-frock'.

Overleaf left: A chocolate brown silk/satin afternoon dress with smocking at the waist, with a matching cape with wide embroidered borders, c. 1905

Overleaf right: 'Dorothy', an 18th century style houserobe of Tyrian silk with smocking at the neck, waist and sleeves. A plate from Liberty's Dress and Decoration, published in 1905

Weldon's Practical Smocking, Second series, 1887 or 1888, stated that:

Smocking is more than ever in vogue this season and is applied to every conceivable article of dress, for not only are children's artistic costumes smocked round the neck, but the fashion is arising for ladies' blouses, and Garibaldi jackets . . . the fullness confined round the waist by a band and buckle . . . tea gowns are smocked across the bust and again at the waist, the intermediate space being left loose and baggy. Some new skirts are made with a breadth of material smocked onto each side to a depth of about a quarter of a yard from the waist . . . Sleeves are smocked at the back below the shoulder or midway between the shoulder and the elbow, and again at the wrists . . . Even sunshades are smocked.

Weldon's recommended 'Liberty silks, Pongee silks and Umritza cashmere' as being especially suitable for smocking, and many items of clothing so adorned were illustrated in Liberty catalogues of the late 1880s and early 1890s.

As well as introducing English-made cashmere, Mr Lasenby Liberty (as he was generally known) was keen to promote British industry, and in 1887, together with Sir Frank Warner, set up the British Silk Association, under the patronage of Princess Mary Adelaide, Duchess of Teck, in an attempt to revive both the hand-woven silks of Spitalfields and the machine-woven silks of Macclesfield, which were facing in-creasing foreign competition, espe-cially from France. Liberty's com-missioned a number of designs, including one of honeysuckle and jas-mine. An article in the *Studio* (vol. I, 1893) by Lasenby Liberty entitled 'Spitalfields Brocades' gave an account of their production, and *The Magazine of Art* (vol. XXII, 1897–8, p. 393 *et seq.*) devoted an article to the 'Revival of the British Silk Industry' featuring Liberty fabrics. Liberty's exhibited some artis-tic gowns at the Paris Exhibition of 1889, and in 1890 opened a branch in Paris at 38 Avenue de l'Opera, taking the 'Soies-Liberty' into the heart of the competition. As the *Silks* catalogue stated, these Soies-Liberty became 'ap-preciated and admired by the *elite* of Continental and American Society'. Among the elite who purchased a Li-berty silk tea gown was the wife of the American millionaire Andrew Carne-gie. It was a gift to her from her husband to celebrate her recovery from a bout of typhoid fever. The dress is now in the Metropolitan Museum of Art, New York.

It would not be feasible to describe the entire vast range of Liberty dress silks and velveteens that were available in the 1890s, but among them were the 'Hercules' silk which had a broken shot effect, the 'Tabdar' satin, woven in Bradford and described as 'suitable for bridesmaids' robes and evening dresses, and the 'Rippana' crape, Yarmouth-woven, in pure silk and suitable for light dress. Their 'Thetis' silk damask was sel-ected for special praise by the *Lady's Pic-torial* in their issue of 17 October 1891:

One is accustomed to expect everything that is exquisite in colour, artistic in design and dainty in texture of the famous firm in Regent Street, but even Messrs. Liberty do not often introduce so uniquely beautiful a fabric as their new 'Thetis' silk damask . . . Nothing could be more appropriate than that the new fabric should be called by the name of a sea-goddess, for in its graceful folds may be traced not only the waving lines and ever varying play of light and shade which rends its distinctive name so apt, but also much of the curious translucency of water.

The Victoria & Albert Museum possesses a full length opera cloak of Thetis

Left: *White satin embroidered wedding dress with lace sleeves and lace at throat, 1906*

Right: *'Marjorie', a child's Empire style velvet coat and hat. From* Dress and Decoration, *1905*

brocade, in the 'Cascade' pattern, in a design that was called 'Pepita'.

The Queen (21 September 1901), was equally enthusiastic over the Liberty velveteens 'in hues borrowed from nature' which suggested 'endless possibilities in the way of tea gowns, dinner dresses, opera cloaks . . . and picturesque frocks for children of all ages'.

Gilbert and Sullivan

Not only were the Liberty silks, cashmeres and velvets designated as 'Art Fabrics' used for ladies and children's fashions, but many of the costumes for the Gilbert and Sullivan operas were made from these materials, some of them in Liberty's workrooms. The Liberty fabrics were used in *Patience* in 1881, the aesthetic dresses being designed by Gilbert himself, in *Iolanthe* in 1882 and *The Mikardo* in 1885. Nearly all the programmes for the Gilbert and Sullivan light operas at the Savoy Theatre included coloured advertisements for Liberty Art Fabrics and other goods, and these are preserved in the Theatre Museum at Covent Garden.

Liberty's also provided costumes for fancy dress parties and amateur dramatics. Two such costumes remain in the possession of the Liberty family, both bearing the label 'Liberty & Co., Artistic and Historic Costume Studio, 222, Regent Street'. One is made from Liberty's 'Hop and Ribbon' silk damask (which was registered in 1892) and green velvet, trimmed with bands of silk embroidery enhanced with iridescent glass beads. It is in a late mediaeval style and may have been worn on informal occasions as well as for dressing up. The other is a robe in the form of a flowing coat in silk brocade over a green-gold satin dress, both edged with green plush. This dates from about 1905.

The *Studio* magazine, founded in 1893, inaugurated Prize Competitions and in 1895, in their Series 'A', *Designs for Industrial Purposes*, one of the set

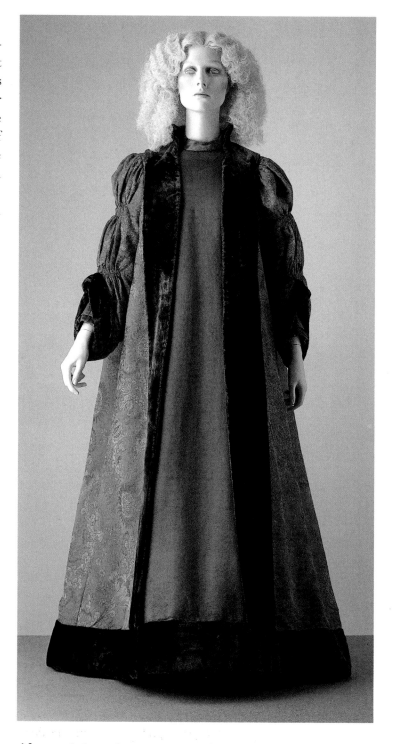

Above: Robe and surcoat with velvet trim, late 1890s

subjects was a design which should include one or more draped female figures and the following lettering: 'LIBERTY' ART FABRICS for Dresses and Furniture, Beautiful and Inexpensive. Patterns post free'. The specified size, landscape shape, was 10 inches by $3\frac{3}{4}$ inches, and the first prize was 5 guineas, the prize designs to be the property of Liberty & Co., who reserved the right to purchase any of the other submitted designs at a price not exceeding one guinea. The first prize was awarded to a competitor under the pseudonym of 'DOCK' who submitted a drawing of a girl, seated on the floor, examining the end of a bolt of cloth. This was used on the back cover of

Left: '*Amelia*', *an Empire style evening gown with a coat in Orion silk, 1905*

Right: '*Marion*', *a Directoire style visiting coat in Orion satin, 1905*

Liberty's *Silks* catalogue, and was obviously an economic way of obtaining a good drawing, while at the same time encouraging new talent.

It was in 1905 that Liberty's published their most lavish costume catalogue, *Dress and Decoration*, a series of twelve coloured plates, reproduced from watercolours by H.E. Howarth, showing the costumes in typical Liberty room settings. Each plate was accom-

panied by a brief description, enclosed in a decorative border, both border and typeface echoing William Morris's Kelmscott Press, adding to the artistic effect of the whole publication.

Each of the costumes was given a woman's name, and most of the settings were in the typical Liberty 'arts and crafts' style, with a strong Glasgow influence in the motifs. Three Empire styles were included: 'Amelia', an Orion silk evening gown and silk velvet coat, with appliqué and embroidery in silk and velvet; 'Helen', a tea gown in flowered crepe-de-Chine with sleeves

Left: Brown velveteen dress in 'Stuart' style. 'Stuart' dresses date from 1908

Right: *'Josephine', an Empire style gown from Liberty's* Dress and Decoration

and neck drapery in Dalghali crape; and 'Josephine', an evening dress in silk crape with hand embroidery in blue and green. Only one outdoor garment was included – 'Marion', a Directoire visiting coat in pale green Orion satin with a wide square hand-embroidered collar and cuffs. Adaptations of English 17th

Above: *'Jacqueline', a French 15th century style velveteen indoor gown with silk crepe sash and tucked net collar*

and 18th century costumes featured in 'Henrietta', a 'Charles II' home gown; 'Cecilia', an English 17th century evening gown smocked at the waist and neck; and 'Nerissa', an early 18th century dress and tea jacket. The two mediaeval styles were of French inspiration, 'Jacqueline', based on 15th century costume with a tucked embroidered net collar and jewelled headband, and 'Iseult', a flowing evening gown of velvet with gauze sleeves derived from 14th century costume. 'Hera', described as an 'Ancient Greek Evening Gown' of Nitas silk with cross bands embroidered in pearls and silver, was given a more formal Louis Quinze setting. The last plate showed two children's costumes, 'Freda', a 'Dutch child' frock of white satin with matching cap, and 'Marjorie', an Empire style velvet coat with an ostrich feather trimmed hat – standing by a Compton Pottery garden ornament.

Burberrys

Such costumes were to have a marked influence on women's dress. Burberrys, of the Haymarket, London, Paris, New York and Buenos Aires, renowned for their raincoats, were, a few years later, to emulate Liberty's in producing a colour brochure entitled *Burberry Colour Melody* to introduce their 'Melody Silks', with a lady in suitably artistic dress, very similar to that of Liberty's, on the cover. To explain the title, the brochure stated:

As melody flatters the ear with sweet sounds, so it is possible to gratify the eye by pleasing effects of colour. The analogy between sound and colour is close . . . Even technological terminology becomes interchangeable, and as we talk of loud or quiet colours, so, with poetic licence, we can use the expression "Colour Melody". Burberrys apply the principles of musical harmony to every detail of dress.

A double-page colour spread had a very artistic photograph of a draped silk fringed shawl, a fur hat and a tweed hat, both adorned with feathers, which was captioned 'Burberry Colour Melody Silk with Natural Plumes and Gamefeather Tweed'.

Liberty went even further in not only supplying artistic costumes for their customers, but in ensuring that their staff were also artistically attired; the 'shopwalkers' wore medieval style dresses, in purple or brown velvet, with embroidered motifs outlining the low square neck and simulating a medieval girdle. It is not known exactly when this practice was introduced, but it was discontinued in 1932.

A fitting comment on Liberty costume is contained in a letter written by George Bernard Shaw to the actress Janet Abchurch, dated Christmas Day 1900, referring to her role in the first performance of his play, *Captain Brassbound's Conversion*, presented by the Stage Society at the Strand Theatre on 16 December 1900. 'You played the whole part', he wrote, 'as far as comedy went, with your dress tucked between your knees. Of the dress itself I say nothing, for we must do what we can afford in that way, not what we like; but although you solved the difficulty of looking well on ARTISTIC lines — on LIBERTY LINES — on simple, sensible lines, such lines are quite wrong for Lady Cecily, who would associate that sort of dressing with Fitzjohn's Avenue and professional people who don't go to Church'.

An insight into the workings of Liberty's costume department was given by a Mrs Sparks, who was born in 1884, and worked for Liberty's from 1897–1910. She was interviewed in 1975 in connection with the Centenary Exhibition at the Victoria & Albert Museum. Although only 13, she heard of a vacancy at Liberty for an apprentice dressmaker, and sat an exam which enabled her to apply for the job. She travelled every day by horse-drawn cab from her home in Finsbury Park to the Liberty workshops in Euston Road. She worked from 8.30 a.m. to 7.0 p.m., Monday to Friday, and from 8.30 a.m. to 1.0 p.m. on Saturday, for which she received a wage of 2/6 a week, rising to 4/- after one year. During the latter part of her career, she visited country houses to fit customers with their frocks and ball gowns, and she remembers working on the dress of the Lady Mayoress of London who, on her wedding, had had eight bridesmaids all dressed in Liberty mauve crepe-de-Chine, trimmed with amethysts. According to Mrs Sparks, there were five fitters in the room where she worked and twenty girls to each table in some of the other rooms — one table for sleeves, one for bodices, one for skirts, etc. Much hand-sewing was involved on frilled and ruched taffeta, putting ruched trimmings on velvet gowns, and sewing on lace trimmings. When she left in 1910 her salary was one guinea.

Another lady who worked briefly for Liberty was a Miss Amy Kotze, who was interviewed by Shirley Bury at the age of 92 in 1976. She was born in South Africa but her family came to England, and

Above: '*Nerissa*', *an 18th century style silk dress with a velveteen jacket, 1905*

after a Convent School education, she studied art at Sydenham. In 1907, at the age of 23 she walked into Liberty's and asked for a job. She earned 15/- a week, working from 8.30 a.m. to 6.0 p.m. drawing designs for embroidery on the trains of dresses, and starting off the work for the embroideresses. She left Liberty's after a few years, but influenced by the artistic, reformed dresses there, made herself a loose tunic, which was much admired by her friends. She then made a dress for the suffragette leader, Mrs Pankhurst, and shortly afterwards set up on her own as a dressmaker. After the First World War, she found that her trade was killed by 'off-the-peg' dresses, and she then founded a gallery in Great Marlborough Street, called the Little Gallery, just round the corner from Liberty's, where she sold the work of artist craftsmen, as well as her own, and exhibited the work of artists including Jacob Epstein and Henri Gaudier-Brzeska. It was, however, her experience at Liberty's that launched her on her career.

Embroidery

The latter half of the 19th century was to see a revival of the art of embroidery, which had been debased by the deadening influence of Berlin woolwork, and Liberty's were to play an important part in this revival.

The first embroideries sold by Liberty's were Eastern imports, such as Japanese *fukusas*, or gift wrappings embroidered in coloured silks and gold thread; fine woollen Indian embroidered shawls from Kashmir, Lahore, Amritsar and Delhi; and Chinese silk shawls, embroidered in white and coloured silks with long silk fringes. To these were soon added embroidered curtains from Algiers, Turkish and Persian embroidered table covers and hangings, which were supplemented by a variety of European embroideries, including items described as antique. In 1877 the South Kensington Museum purchased three 18th century Spanish

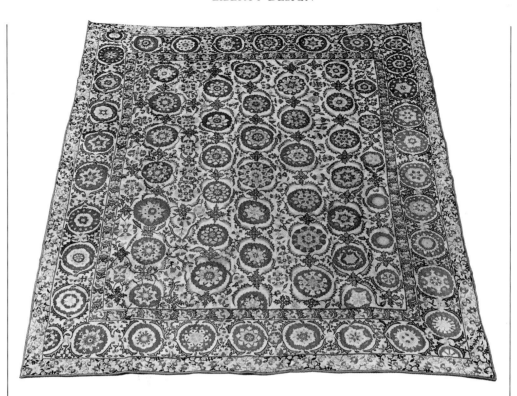

Above: *A 19th century Bokhara hanging embroidered in coloured silks. Imported by Liberty & Co.*

embroidered coverlets, and an 18th century Portuguese embroidered coverlet, along with some Persian and Caucasian carpets, and in 1891 the Museum purchased an Italian 17th century embroidered chasuble, as well as antique Turkish velvet, Italian brocade and 18th century costume.

In November 1885 Liberty's sponsored an exhibition of 'Ancient and Modern Eastern Art and other Embroideries' and a number of exhibitions of 'Art Embroideries' throughout the 1890s, including one of 'Modern Turkish Embroideries' in 1892.

The catalogue of the 1885 Exhibition stated, in the Introduction, that:

. . . the 'Liberty' School of Embroidery has now completed the first year of its existence and during the twelve months many elaborate pieces of work have been executed. Fortunately, for business purposes, but unfortunately for the present exhibition, a press of private orders has prevented us being able to exhibit any large examples.

However, the exhibition did include typical pieces of 'art embroidery' such as mantel borders and fireplace curtains in adaptations of Chinese designs on velveteen, Japanese design folding screens, handkerchief sachets, tussore silk embroidered table covers, and table covers and sofa backs in Langdale linen.

The Langdale linen industry had been

Above: *A 19th century Turkish embroidery. Liberty's imported much of this work*

established in the year of the exhibition, with the encouragement of John Ruskin, to provide employment in the Lake District hamlets of Great and Little Langdale, Elterwater and Stile; characteristically Arthur Liberty supported this philanthropic enterprise.

Liberty's associations with Thomas Wardle, whose wife had founded the Leek Embroidery Society in 1879, inspired the firm to sell lengths of cotton printed with a single colour outline pattern to be used as a basis of embroidery by the home embroideress. The resulting embroideries, worked in specially dyed 'Art' silks were used as screen panels and as curtains. The selvedge of one such design of meandering stems bearing peonies, tulips, daffodils and other flowers and leaves was printed 'Liberty & Co., Regent Street, London Registered', and dates from the 1890s.

The most original of the Liberty embroideries, however, were those commissioned from Ann Macbeth (1875–1948) in the art nouveau style of the Glasgow School, which included cushion covers and decorative panels, some with typical Glasgow School motifs, in appliqué and embroidery, others with pictorial designs of ladies in artistic costume, in the manner of contemporary book illustrations. Ann Macbeth, who studied at the Glasgow School of Art from 1897–9, was appointed as an assistant to Jessie Newbery, who had established em-

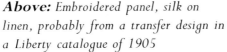

Above: *Embroidered panel, silk on linen, probably from a transfer design in a Liberty catalogue of 1905*

Above: *Mahogany firescreen, c. 1900, with an embroidered panel. Possibly purchased from Liberty's*

broidery classes at the school in 1894. She was one of the outstanding embroideresses of the 20th century, both as an artist and as a teacher. Her book on *Educational Needlecraft*, published in 1911, was to revolutionize the teaching of embroidery in schools throughout the country. Some of her designs for Liberty's could be bought ready-worked, but many were adapted as transfers for embroidery to be used on both dress and furnishings, designs that continued to be featured in Liberty catalogues until the out-

break of the First World War.

Most of the embroidery designs were sold in the form of transfers, which had to be ironed on to the fabric, and the designs were illustrated in outline on a much reduced scale. The transfers could be ordered by post, but those who were able to visit the shop for themselves were given free advice on the choice and arrangement of colours. A lesson in the techniques of embroidery could be arranged by appointment. The Liberty embroidery silks were described as being in 'colours reproduced from notable examples of Ancient Embroidery. They excel in quality and tone'. The range included designs for the decoration of blotters, firescreens, photograph frames, tea-cosies, night-dress cases, sofa and cushion covers, and narrow borders which could be used for both furnishing and dress. Designs for the yoke of a child's dress were included, and a few ecclesiastical designs for the ends of stoles. The pictorial designs, which it was suggested could be used for frieze repeats as well as cushion covers, included Little Bo-Peep, Una and the Lion, Dutch landscape and stylized tree designs, which were similar to those for the wallpaper friezes. Virtually the same range of designs appear in the *Transfer Designs for Application to Needlework*, of about 1904, *Designs for Needlework* of 1905, and *Designs for Needlework* of about 1909. The latter catalogue also includes a colour illustration of an Indo-Portuguese coverlet in the Victoria & Albert Museum, together with a number of designs adapted from it, the result in fact being designs that are very close to William Morris. There is also one 'Jacobean' style design for a sofa, some interlaced Celtic designs, but the Glasgow style of art nouveau predominates.

About 1912 an attractive range of blotters, photograph frames and the like was introduced. They were covered in natural linen and embroidered with designs of stylized roses in silk and metal thread, with stems in appliqué of black silk ribbon. The designer is not known, but the inspiration was clearly that of the Glasgow School.

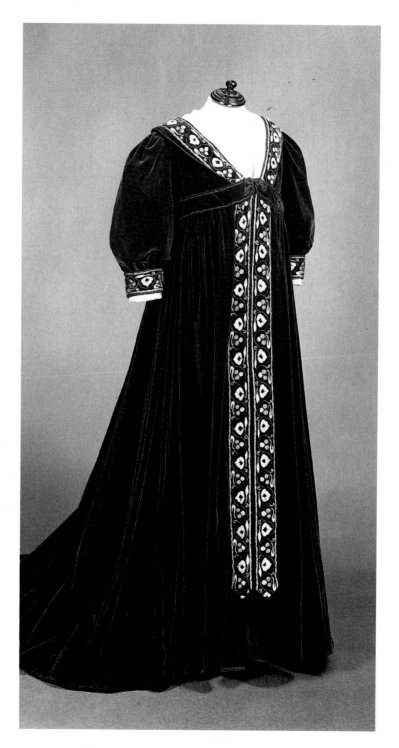

Above: *Liberty purple velvet dress with hand embroidered borders. c. 1900*

Three examples of Moorcroft's 'Pomegranate' design,
sold by Liberty's as 'Murena Ware'

60

Chapter Three

CERAMICS AND GLASS

In the early days, Liberty's specialized in Far Eastern ceramics, both antique and modern. However, before long, they began to seek out and stock the best examples of contemporary English and Continental art pottery. Doulton of Lambeth, William Moorcroft, and Max Läuger of Germany were among the potters who produced designs especially for Liberty's. The glass included 'Clutha' glass designed by Christopher Dresser, the French art glass of Eugene Rousseau and Ernest Leveille, and the iridescent glass by Lötz of Austria. The firm of James Powell & Sons of Whitefriars supplied both table glass and glass for mounting in silver and pewter.

Above: *Two 'Barum' ware jugs by C.H. Brannam of Barnstaple, 1900–1910*

For the first few years Liberty's sold mainly imported Oriental ceramics, both antique and modern. The firm called the antique blue and white 'Old Nankin China', and this was relatively expensive with prices up to 30 guineas; however, they also sold modern Canton dishes for as little as 6d. Both modern and antique Japanese ceramics were also sold, together with a more limited range of old Dutch delft and Grès de Flandres, all of which appealed to aesthetic tastes. Indian and Near Eastern pottery was also available, including earthenware vases and plates made by the Bombay School of Art.

'Barum' ware

By the early 1880s, although they continued to import Oriental wares, Liberty's began to turn to both British and Continental art pottery. One of the earliest associations with an art pottery was with that of Charles Hubert Brannam (1855–1937), which was known as 'Barum' ware. C.H. Brannam, after studying at art school, took over his father's pottery in Barnstaple, Devon, in 1879, and transformed the traditional country 'peasant' pottery into a stylish range of art pottery which was sold by Liberty from 1882 until the late 1930s. The earliest pieces had typically aesthetic designs of birds and blossom, with a somewhat Japanese influence, incised through coloured slips on a red earthenware body. This range was followed by designs of grotesque fish and marine motifs, including vases with dragon handles, in predominating shades of blue, green and brown. From about 1900 Liberty's commissioned much simpler designs of 'Barum' ware, including toilet sets in plain blue and green, together with vases and tankards with simple, circular motifs; art nouveau designs of heart-shaped leaves and sinuous stems outlined in slip, owl bowls and 'motto' ware. The bases of these items are normally inscribed 'C.H. Brannam/ Barum/N. Devon/ Made for Liberty & Co.' and often have the registration number Rd. 44561, dating from 1886, which the firm continued to use well into the 20th century, considering it as their trademark.

Another Devon pottery patronized by Liberty was the Aller Vale Art Pottery, situated between Newton Abbot and Kingskerswell. The pottery had been making simple brown ware since 1865 and, under the direction of John Phillips, began making decorative wares with *sgraffito* decoration through coloured slip from 1887. Their speciality became motto-ware, which was sold not only in the resorts of South Devon but all over the country, including Liberty's.

Somewhat similar to the early 'Barum' ware, but perhaps closer to the Linthorpe Pottery designed by Christopher Dresser, was the Bretby Art Pottery of Woodville, Derbyshire. It was established in 1883 by William Ault and Henry Tooth, who had been manager of the Linthorpe Pottery. The Liberty *Yule-Tide Gifts Catalogue* of December 1888 features a number of Bretby flower pots in shaded colours, including one with a dragon design, and a green shaded pampas grass or palm holder.

Well-known potteries, such as Doulton of Lambeth, also made special designs for Liberty's, including tall stoneware candlesticks decorated with stylized honesty, an art nouveau motif which also occurs on Liberty furniture. These candlesticks, and others made for Liberty, bear the normal Doulton marks and 'Made for Liberty & Co'.

Liberty's were also to give encouragement to lesser known art potteries, including items from the Farnham Pottery, run by A. Harris & Sons, selling large quantities of their wares which included jugs, vases and candlesticks, under the general name of 'Green Ware'. Another range of artistic pottery, made by Wardle & Co., Washington Works, Hanley (renamed Wardle Art Pottery Co. Ltd. in 1910) and marked 'Made for Liberty & Co.', had incised designs of lobsters and other sea creatures on a mottled green ground, or flowers in coloured slip on a mottled blue ground; the former was marketed by Liberty under the name of 'Heros', the latter under the name of 'Hadcote'.

William Moorcroft

These all harmonized with both the Anglo-Japanese and the oak furniture sold by Liberty's, but Liberty's also provided suitable ceramics for their more elegant furniture, much of it designed by William Moorcroft (1872–1945). After studying at the Burslem School of Art and the National Art Training School at South Kensington, William Moorcroft obtained his Art Masters Certificate in 1897. He was then offered a post as

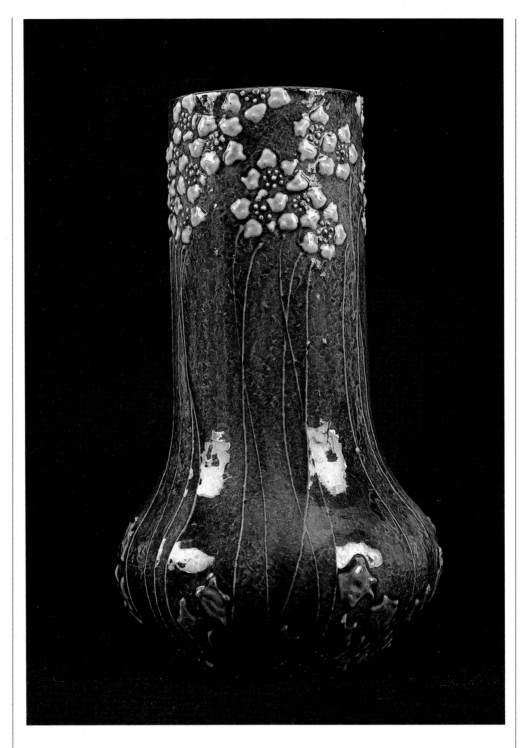

A 'Hadcote' vase with raised slip design,
made for Liberty's by Wardle & Co., c. 1905

designer and organizer of a new art pottery department set up by James Macintyre and Company of the Washington Works, Burslem. By 1898 he had introduced a new range of art pottery called 'Florian Ware', with art nouveau floral designs, in which the flowers, although stylized, were usually identifiable. The 'Florian' ware was made mainly in shades of blue or green, sometimes on a cream ground, and the motifs were outlined in white slip.

Within two years Moorcroft was producing pieces marked 'Made for Liberty & Co.', and had formed a close friendship with Lasenby Liberty and his wife (a friendship that was to endure until Liberty's death in 1917), continuing to supply pottery to Liberty's until his own death in 1945.

The Liberty & Co. *Yule-Tide Gifts* catalogue for 1901 carries a full-page advertisement for Florian ware, showing shallow two-handled bowls, elongated and squat vases, tobacco and tea jars with peacock-feather designs as well as floral patterns. The ware was described as 'an exceedingly decorative English Pottery. The designs are delicately treated, and are in a cream colour relieved with olive green. The elegant forms in many specimens are reminiscent of Pompeian models, others are adapted from the later Italian and contemporary schools.' Gilding was sometimes added from about 1903. A new pattern of trees in a landscape was introduced in 1902 with the name 'Hazledene', which has the facsimile signature 'W. Moorcroft' and 'Made

Below: Florian ware vases by William Moorcroft, first sold by Liberty's in 1898

for Liberty & Co./Rd. 397964'. A year later, the 'Claremont' design was introduced, with the same marks as before but with the registered number 420081. It has a rather strange design of toadstools. The Liberty *Bric-a-brac* catalogue of about 1905 states that 'The motif . . . and the name were suggested by a peculiar kind of fungi growing in the woods on the estate of the Duchess of Albany'. Other registered designs for Liberty were the 'Poppy' (1902), and the 'Tudor Rose' (1904), and the 'Red Flamminian' and 'Green Flamminian' registered in 1905. The Flamminian ware came in a wide variety of shapes, and was monochrome red or green decorated only by small circular motifs. The 'Bara Ware' design, also introduced about 1905, had delicate swags of

small pink roses on a cream ground, and was very close to Moorcroft's '18th Century Pattern', which had festoons of roses tied with blue ribbon.

The 'Bara Ware' pattern was used for toilet sets, as well as for vases, and harmonized with a 'Cymric' silver toilet set designed by Jessie M. King, which was registered in 1906. Lustred pottery by Moorcroft was also sold by Liberty, and large quantities of Moorcroft's 'Pomegranate' design,

Opposite: *Moorcroft Blue Tableware*

Below: *A selection of Moorcroft's red and green Flamminian ware. The blue vases date from 1914, after Moorcroft had moved his pottery to Cobridge*

introduced about 1910, was sold under the name 'Murena ware', together with the 'Spanish Flower' design of about 1911. All these designs were produced by James Macintyre until 1913, when Moorcroft left to set up his own factory at Cobridge, taking with him most of those who had worked for him. The old patterns were kept in production and new ones were added. It was in 1913 that Moorcroft launched a range of tableware, with a mid-blue glaze with a dark blue speckle that was known as 'Moorcroft Blue'. It was sold by Liberty's and also used in their Tudor Tea Rooms in the 1920s.

As well as decorative ceramics and tablewares, Liberty's also offered an extensive range of garden ornaments made in terracotta, with Celtic decoration. This was made by Mrs G.F. Watts (Mary Fraser-Tytler), who set up a pottery at Compton, near Guildford in Surrey, around 1902. It was made in what was described as 'frost proof earthenware, red or grey, that with exposure assumes an interesting old-world and weather stained appearance'.

Below: *A pair of earthenware jardinieres and stands by Archibald Knox*

There were shrub pots, flower pots, pedestals, window boxes, bird baths, sundials, fountains, garden seats and benches and terrace balustrades. Her work for Liberty's earned her gold and silver medals from the Royal Botanic Society and The Royal Horticultural Society. The 'Tara' garden seat, decorated with interlaced Celtic motifs, and the 'Athena' and 'Alcuin' sundials, illustrated in W. Shaw Sparrow's *Hints on House Furnishing* (London, 1909) are typical examples. Liberty & Co. also sold, although not so extensively, similar garden pottery made by Owen Carter at Poole in Dorset, a fine example of which is now in the Cecil Higgins Museum, Bedford.

Max Läuger

Not content with merely seeking out the best of English art pottery and tablewares, Liberty's also looked to the Continent. Outstanding among the Continental pottery sold by Liberty's was that made by Max Läuger (1864–1952), who was Art Director of the Kandern ceramic factory at Karlsrühe from 1892–1913. A painter, architect, sculptor and designer, as well as a ceramist, Läuger studied in Paris and Italy, and from 1885–1898 lectured at Karlsrühe University. His ceramics are characterized by stylized floral designs in coloured slips, in art nouveau style. Liberty's. were the first to import his wares into England and one of their catalogues of about 1890 describes them as 'Beautiful shapes with graceful structuresque decoration applied upon a surface of singularly fine tex-

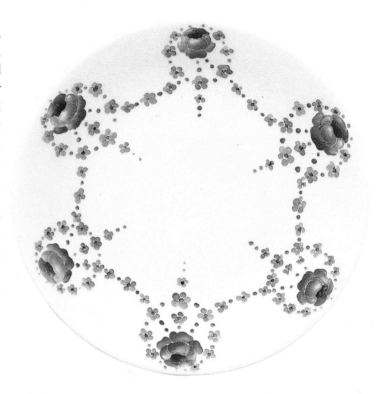

Above: *A 'Bara Ware' plate by William Moorcroft*

ture . . . Exceedingly effective for Sideboard Decoration, Overmantels etc.' Examples of Läuger's pottery were bought from Liberty's by the Victoria & Albert Museum in 1898 and 1900.

Lustre ware

The lustred pottery of the Zsolnay factory of Pècs (Fünfkirchen), which was also art nouveau, was sold by Liberty's around the turn of the century. A type of tin glazed Dutch pottery, made by a number of firms and marketed under the name of 'Breda' ware was made exclusively for Liberty's from about 1908. The bases are usually marked 'Liberty & Co/Made in Holland' and the pottery has stylized plant and geometrical ornament with a Javanese influence, usually painted in blue and yellow on a dark green or brown ground.

The earthenware of the Cantigalli factory in Florence, which specialized in the revival of Italian renaissance majolica and Hispano-Moresque wares with lustred decoration, was also sold by Liberty's in the late 1880s and 1890s.

Clutha glass

Compared to ceramics, relatively little British glass was sold by Liberty's, apart from the 'Clutha' glass designed by Christopher Dresser for James Couper and Sons of Glasgow. It was introduced in the late 1880s and described by Liberty's as 'Decorative, Quaint, Original and Artistic'. The name 'Clutha' was derived from the ancient Celtic name for the River Clyde which runs through Glasgow, and much of the glass, like its name, was consciously archaic, being deliberately bubbled and streaked. It was made in a variety of colours, including green, pink, amber and brown, with striations in white, blue and red, sometimes in controlled festoons, sometimes in random, swirling patterns, with patches of aventurine. The shapes often followed

Below: Four vases by Max Läuger, decorated in coloured slips, c. 1898

Above: 'Clutha' glass vase by Christopher Dresser, late 1880s

the forms of antique glass, particularly Egyptian, Roman and Near Eastern, the shapes that Dresser admired and illustrated in his *Principles of Decorative Design*, published in 1873.

One particularly attractive vase with a long, slender neck was based on a 17th century Persian rose-water sprinkler in the South Kensington Museum, and others echoed the forms of some Indian glass acquired by the Museum in 1888. This 'Clutha' glass designed by Dresser and sold by Liberty's was acid etched on the base of each vessel with the words 'CLUTHA/DESIGNED BY C.D./REGISTERED' in a circle enclosing the Liberty 'Lotus' trademark. In 1896 a new range of 'Clutha' glass was introduced, designed by the Glasgow architect George

Walton (1867–1933), who also designed furniture for Liberty. This was usually green, with large patches of gold or copper aventurine, and in rather more conventional, squatter shapes; it was also made to be mounted in 'Tudric' pewter. The Dresser 'Clutha' glass, however, continued to be sold, certainly as late as 1900.

In 1902, Liberty's introduced an attractive range of table glass in 'new and beautiful forms' to which they gave the name 'Dewdrop' glass. It first appears in *The Yule-Tide Gifts* catalogue of 1902. The colourless glass had applied 'blobs' or 'tears' of lead crystal glass with trails reaching the base of the body of a decanter, or the stem of a glass. The first range included claret or hock, champagne, sherry, port and liqueur glasses, half and three-quarter pint glasses, and wine, spirit and liqueur decanters. The 1903 *Yule-Tide Gifts* catalogue shows a considerable extension of the range, including jugs, flower vases in clear and green glass, celery glasses, grog bottles and new shapes for claret and hock decanters with elongated twisted stoppers, all similarly decorated with the crystal 'blobs'. Liberty's described the glass as 'An English Made Novelty', but no manufacturer was given. It seems likely, however, that it was made by James Powell & Sons of Whitefriars, who also supplied glass for mounting in the 'Cymric' silver and 'Tudric' pewter.

Above: *'Clutha' glass bowl by Christopher Dresser, c. 1895*

Johan Lötz Witwe

About the same time, Liberty began importing the iridescent glass made by Johan Lötz Witwe of Klostermühle, in Austria. This first appears in their 1903 *Yule-Tide Gifts* catalogue as 'A NEW LUSTROUS GLASS, glinting and glowing with opalesque radiance in rich metallic colourings'. The glass had an amber or ruby ground with bluish green metallic splashes, like the iridescence on butterfly wings – in fact, the manufacturers named it 'Papillon' glass. The range consisted of two-handled flower bowls, flower vases, often with dimpled bodies and lobed frilled rims, and smaller vases described as 'cabinet specimens'. Somewhat earlier, crackled glass by the French potter and glassmaker Eugène Rousseau (1827–1891)

Above: Four pieces of iridescent glass by Johann Lötz Witwe of Klostermuhle, Austria. The second piece from the left, with two handles and a pattern of leaves around the neck, is mounted in pewter. Lötz glass first appears in Liberty's Yule-tide Gifts *catalogue of 1903*

had been sold by Liberty, glass which harmonized with the Chinese and Japanese wares of the Eastern Bazaar. Particularly impressive were vases in sculptured forms, with elephant head handles, in thick, chunky glass with an internal crackle, coloured a glowing shade of pink. After Rousseau's death in 1891, the glass was made by his assistant, Ernest Baptiste Leveillé. Unfortunately, most of their glass is unsigned.

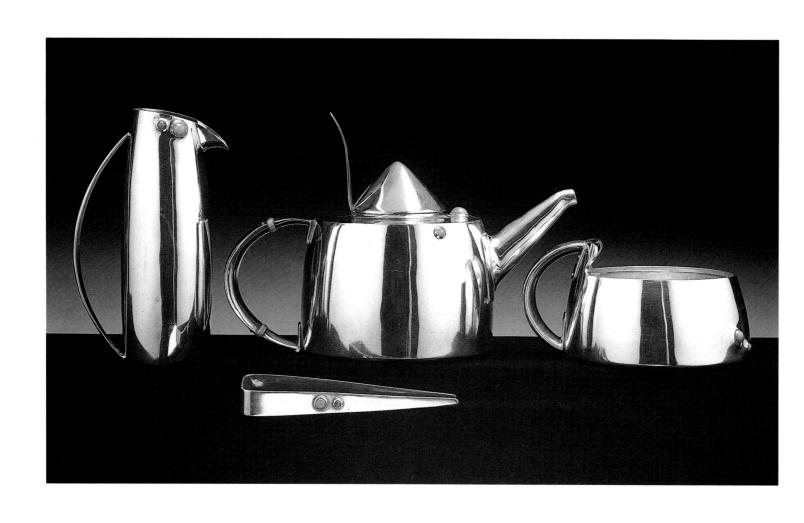

'Cymric' silver tea set by Archibald Knox, c. 1903

Chapter Four

SILVER, JEWELLERY AND METALWORK

Before introducing their own ranges of silver, jewellery, pewter and other metalwork, Liberty's relied on foreign importations; among them were Japanese bronzes, Chinese 'curios' and brass wares from Indian bazaars. Next, they introduced English beaten copper and brass, including objects designed by Christopher Dresser and John Pearson. Then, in 1899, came their highly original 'Cymric' silver and jewellery, to be followed, in 1901, by the equally splendid 'Tudric' pewter. Both ranges were outstanding examples of the Liberty style, with designs from the Silver Studio and from the hand of Archibald Knox.

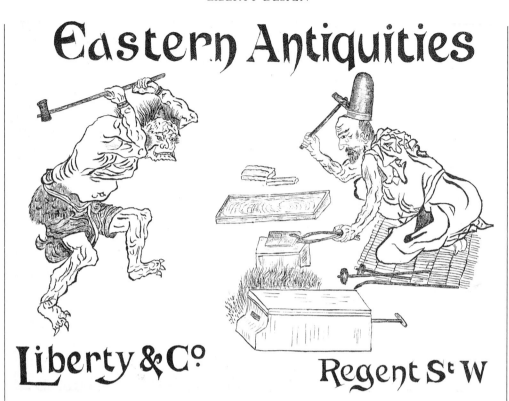

As with textiles and embroidery, the first examples of metalwork sold by Liberty's were of Oriental manufacture. Japanese products predominated, including fine bronze vases, some with diaper ornament, some with elephant head handles, others encircled with dragons. There were also naturalistic bronze animals, and bronze and brass candlesticks, adorned with lions and dragons. Especially popular, possibly because they were cheaper, were white metal candlesticks with a bronze finish, the stems in the form of frogs, one sitting and one standing on waterlily leaves.

Among the most expensive items, described as 'cabinet pieces', were iron cabinets, damascened in gold, specially commissioned from leading Japanese craftsmen including Komai of Kyoto and Konoike of Yokohama. Fine examples of *cloisonné* enamel, including vases with designs of flowers, birds, dragons and fishes, and saké kettles and bowls, were also to be found. Most items were of contemporary manufacture, but there were also some antiques such as *tsuba* or sword guards. Inexpensive items were also available for, as *The Furniture Gazette* reported on 19 October 1878, 'the most progressive tradesman in Regent Street (i.e. Liberty) sells Japanese *bric-à-brac*'. Their *Eastern Art* catalogue of 1881 advertised their prices as ranging from 1/- to £500.

Above: *The cover of* Eastern Antiquities, *one of Liberty's very early catalogues*

The Chinese metalwork, which included incense burners and jewellery, was described in the Liberty catalogue as 'curios'. Liberty also imported a wide range of bric-à-brac from India. The Indian Pavilion at the Paris Exhibition of 1889 included a selection of their stock of Indian metalwork, including Bombay inlaid work, brass ware from Benares and Moradabad and copper bottles and trays from Kashmir, the latter for use as tea trays.

A vast range of metalwork from the Near East was mostly bazaar work from Damascus and Cairo, catering for the fashionable 'smoking rooms', and including mosque lamps, ewers, coffee-pots and trays.

As well as selling Japanese and Chinese enamels, Liberty's sold cloisonné enamel designed by the English artist Clement John Heaton (1861–1940), the son of the founder of Heaton, Butler and Bayne, stained glass manufacturers and decorators. On his father's death in 1882, Heaton succeeded his father in the firm but left after a dispute in 1885. He designed metalwork and light fittings for A.H. Mackmurdo's Century Guild and developed a speciality in cloisonné enamel, setting up his own firm: Heaton's Cloisonné Mosaics Ltd. He moved his workshop to Neuchâtel in Switzerland in the early 1890s, but continued to supply examples for Liberty's. Two fine copper salvers with outlines in brass filled in with coloured mastic, which he called 'Chatoyant enamel', were purchased by the Victoria & Albert Museum from Liberty's in 1899. The larger one has a diameter

Above: *A beaten copper charger with a Viking ship and an enormous fish in the centre, surrounded by a border of four fish. Made by John Pearson in 1898*

of 59cm (23ins) with a design of stylized scrolls surrounded by a border of yellow flowers and green leaves, the smaller is 44cm (17ins) across and has a large central yellow flower surrounded by green leaves.

John Pearson

From about 1892, Liberty's sold circular beaten copper dishes or plaques executed by John Pearson, which appear in their catalogues on sideboards and hanging shelves. Pearson was already a skilled craftsman and designer when he joined C.R. Ashbee's Guild of Handicraft in 1888 but, following some disagreements, he resigned in 1892 to work on his own. The Pearson dishes usually had a centre embossed with a galleon, a grotesque beast or a peacock, surrounded by a broad border of fish or dolphins, or scrolling floral and plant forms. His inspiration seems to have been English repoussé silver dishes of the 1660s and German and Flemish brass dishes of the 15th and 16th century. He also decorated ceramic dishes, bowls and tiles with similar motifs which were close to those of the potter William De Morgan (1839–1917), for whom he may have worked earlier as a tile painter.

Besides selling beaten copper items by professionals, such as John Pearson, Liberty's also sold amateur work produced by members of the Home Arts and Industries Association, an organisation formed in 1883 under the presidency of Lord Brownlow, with the writer Walter Besant (1836–1901) as the Treasurer. The founders had been inspired by the teachings of John Ruskin and the belief in the importance of manual training. Classes were started all over England, and in Ireland, and as well as metalwork, the members practised

Below: A 'Kordofan' candlestick in polished brass with a wooden handle

Above: *Japanese silver teapot by Konoike of Yokohama*

inset with turquoise or ceramic plaques, or decorated with enamel, and similar designs were executed in pewter.

The only metalwork designed by Christopher Dresser to be sold by Liberty's seems to have been the candlesticks made by Richard Perry & Son of Wolverhampton, which were registered in 1883. They described them as the 'Kordofan candlestick' in 'Liberty Art Colours', without acknowledging the source of design, although 'Dr Dresser's Design' appears on the handle alongside the diamond registration mark. The candlestick had an inverted semi-hemispherical base, with a smaller shallow bowl at the top, linked by a short cylinder, with the curved ebonized handle attached to the base by brass mounts. The metal was painted either in deep turquoise or Venetian red, but could also be bought in plain, polished brass.

Silver

In 1894, five years before he sponsored an exclusive range of English silver and jewellery, Arthur Lasenby Liberty registered a maker's mark, LY & CO., at Goldsmiths' Hall. The entry in the mark book is dated 8 February 1894 and bears his personal signature. It seems that this registration of a Liberty mark was initially solely to exercise his right to recognition as a dealer and importer of silver, complying with the law that required all imported silver goods to be assayed. The Victoria & Albert Museum possesses a Japanese silver teapot, signed by Konoike of Yokohama, with

wood-carving, modelling, leatherwork and embroidery. One of the most successful classes was that run at Yattendon by Mrs Alfred Waterhouse, the wife of the architect, and beaten copper articles, made by the class, were sold by Liberty's in the 1890s.

Another good selling line were wall mirrors with beaten copper or brass surrounds. Some, such as the 'Arendal', had interlaced Celtic motifs, others had floral decoration. The 'Tulip' mirror had a vertical rectangular frame with a repoussé motif of a tulip and leaves on each side. Other mirror frames were

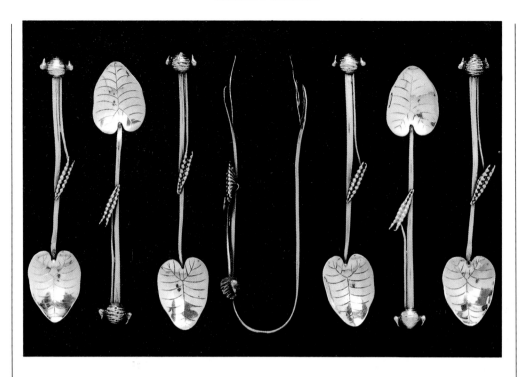

the London import marks for 1896–7 and the maker's mark of LY & CO. Japanese silver spoons, with human and plant motifs recalling the naturalistic designs of the mid-century, were also imported during the 1890s, some bearing the LY & CO. mark. These Japanese goods took their place with the other Oriental imports which had been a Liberty speciality since the foundation of the firm.

The first range of silver and jewellery to be designed and made for Liberty's in England was launched at a small exhibition in the shop in May 1899. It was marketed under the name 'Cymric' which was given to the range by John Llewellyn who had joined Liberty's in 1889 after working for Howell & James, a shop which, like Liberty's, catered for aesthetic tastes. He first worked in the Silk department, and was appointed

Above: Set of six Japanese silver teaspoons and matching sugar tongs imported by Liberty's in 1894

head of the department in 1891, becoming responsible for the commissioning and purchasing of designs. In 1898 he was appointed to the board of directors, retiring in 1935. It seems certain that he was responsible not only for naming the range, but for the initiation. The 1899 exhibition of Cymric Silverwork comprised some eighty pieces from which, as the catalogue stated:

> . . . may be gathered an idea of the nature of the new school of silverwork, of its originality of style, and of its admirable adaptability to articles of both ornament and utility. The silver is not burnished, except as regards an

occasional decorative detail, a shining boss, a quaint bit of hammered ornament in low relief, or what-not, but the soft natural sheen of the metal untouched, the charm of variety being obtained by originality of form, and by the fact that the work is all hand hammered, by which that individuality which is so desirable, and which is an essential condition of the production of art is assured.

The exhibits comprised toilet requisites – hand mirrors, brushes, etc., buckles and clasps, 'graceful vases, sometimes with two or three quaintly shaped handles, squat but shapely sugar bowls, quite original yet not wholly unsuggestive of the old-time *lanx*, or the handled 17th century basons (sic) for heating wine', together with pen trays, spoons, salt cellars and pepper pots, card-cases, matchboxes and cigar-cases.

Liberty's, with their customary lack of modesty, aimed at 'recognition as a characteristic innovation which may identify them with a new *fin-de-siècle* school of art silverwork, marked by an originality of conception and fineness of execution which shall satisfy experts and gratify connoisseurs'.

All the pieces were given romantic sounding names with an archaic ring. The silver bowls were called 'Ostia', 'Edron', 'Edwy', 'Edred', 'Maya', 'Romany', 'Clywin' and 'Cenis'. Among the names for the vases were 'Cyrus', 'Senlac', 'Clytius' and 'Clovis', while 'Walrona', 'Avalon' and 'Idwal' identified the pen trays. Even the teaspoons had names such as 'Egbert' and

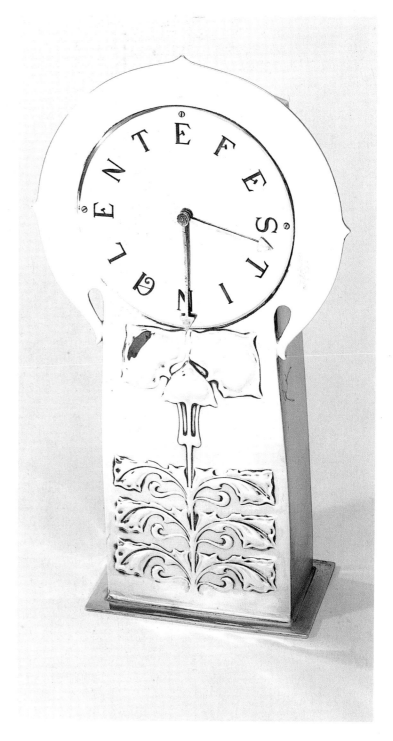

Above: *Liberty 'Cymric' silver clock cast in low relief. 1903*

'Sarepta'. The handles of the 'Sarepta' teaspoons terminated in a stylized leaf design, which in later examples had a green enamel background.

It has not been possible to trace all the items in the first exhibition, nor to identify all the designers, but it is likely that most of them came from the Silver Studio, which at that time was directed by Rex Silver (1879–1965), the son of the founder, Arthur Silver, who died in 1896. A large number of original designs for these early 'Cymric' pieces are in the archives of the Silver Studio, now held by Middlesex Polytechnic. An elegant silver flower vase, of tapering cylindrical form, with a chased irregular linear frieze near the top, and four riveted handles, was called the 'Cyrus', and bears the mark LY & CO. and the London hall-mark for 1899. The design for this and other similar vases appears on a sheet of designs, executed in charcoal and pencil on cartridge paper, inscribed 'Draughts (sic) for Vases' which dates from 1898–9. This, like the designs for three bowls in the first exhibition, the 'Ostia', the 'Maya' and the 'Romany', would appear, on stylistic grounds, to be by Archibald Knox.

Another Silver Studio design for a 'Cymric' silver powder box, with a

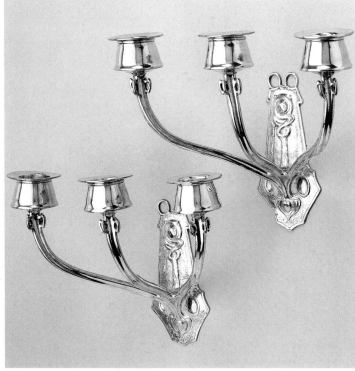

Above: A 'Cymric' silver and enamel frame, probably designed by the Silver Studio, 1901

Below: A pair of Liberty 'Cymric' silver wall sconces, bearing the Birmingham hallmark for 1901

design of birds (a favourite Knox motif) and stylized flowers is annotated in Knox's hand. Whether Knox was actually employed by the Silver Studio, or whether he merely sold his designs to Liberty through the Studio is uncertain. Other designs in the collection, including some for later pieces of 'Cymric' silver and for pewter, are inscribed in the hand of Rex Silver. There is no doubt that he suggested, supervised and criticized all the designs produced by both in-house and freelance designers who worked for the Silver Studio. However, in spite of extensive research by Mark Turner, Keeper of the collection, to what extent he was actually the originator of the designs is unclear. Since many of the designs are in pencil on tracing paper, those inscribed by him may be tracings of an original design by another artist. A Liberty 'Cymric' silver candlestick, the 'Conister', was illustrated in the *Studio* magazine of 1900 (vol. XIX, p. 127), attributed to Rex Silver, but as was customary practice in all 19th century design studios, objects were normally credited to the head of the studio, even if the design emanated from another hand. A number of the designs inscribed by Rex Silver have interlaced Celtic designs showing the influence of Knox, but other more floral designs, including a number for cloak and belt clasps, are more likely to have been by other members of the Silver Studio, notably Harry Napper (1860–1940) and John Illingworth Kay (1870–1950), who both also designed textiles for Liberty's. These floral belt clasps, including the 'Exon', 'Floris'

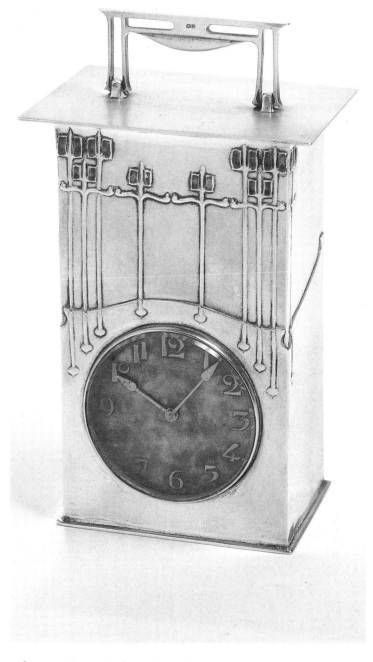

Above: *'Cymric' silver clock, the design attributed to Rex Silver. 1903*

and 'Clyppan' are illustrated, printed in silver, in the 'Liberty' *Yule-Tide Gifts* catalogue of 1899. All the early pieces that have been traced bear a London hall-mark, although the silversmiths who made them have not been identified. In September 1899, however, a new maker's mark, L & CO., in three conjoined lozenges was registered at the Birmingham Assay Office by William Rabone Haseler, in conjunction with two of Liberty's partners, W. Street and J.W. Howe. At the Arts and Crafts Exhibition held in the autumn of 1899, Liberty showed a new range of Cymric silver, all the designers and craftsmen being connected with Birmingham. The designers included Oliver Baker, Bernard Cuzner and A.H. Jones, and the executants were Jessie Jones, Thomas Hodgetts and Charles Povey. It seems likely that they were brought together by William Rabone Haseler, the elder son of William Hair Haseler, the founder of the firm of W.H. Haseler, established as a jewellery concern in 1849.

Until 1901, the Cymric silver appears to have been made both in London and Birmingham, but in that year a new company, Liberty & Co. (Cymric) Ltd., was founded, linking Liberty's and Haseler, who thereafter continued to execute all the silver.

Oliver Baker

Oliver Baker (1856–1939), a painter and etcher who had studied at Birmingham School of Art, produced designs for bowls, boxes and belt clasps, a number of which had an almost exaggerated handmade look, with great strapwork loops of silver forming supports for a bowl, and applied strapwork, escutcheon and scrolling terminals on a shaped rectangular jewel or presentation casket. Smaller items, such as spoons, had strapwork terminals. His belt buckles were usually in the form of open cartouches, or interlaced tendrils, either enamelled or set with turquoise.

Bernard Cuzner

Bernard Cuzner (1877–1956), a silversmith and jeweller, studied at the Victoria Street School of Jewellers and Silversmiths under Arthur Gaskin, one of the most talented 'Arts and Crafts'

Below: *The very popular 'Cymric' silver rose bowl designed by Bernard Cuzner*

jewellers. He designed both silver and jewellery for the 'Cymric' range, including one of their most popular designs, a rose bowl raised on four curving legs on a ring base, the legs continuing upwards as formalized trees and blossoms. The bowl was usually set with turquoises, but occasionally with opals.

Archibald Knox

Undoubtedly the most successful designs for 'Cymric' silver, and for the 'Tudric' pewter, introduced in 1901, were those by Archibald Knox which made an important contribution to the Celtic revival and were instrumental in promoting the 'Liberty Style' at home and abroad. Today his designs are eagerly sought by both museums and private collectors, and attract the highest prices. The identification of his designs, owing to Liberty's policy of anonymity, is often on purely stylistic grounds, except where the object was illustrated under his name in a contemporary periodical, or, in the case of the Arts & Crafts Exhibition of 1903, where acknowledgement of both the designer and maker was mandatory. The problem of identification is further compounded by the fact that Liberty's would often adapt some of his designs or put his motifs on objects designed by others.

Archibald Knox was born on 2 April 1864 at Cronkbourne in the Isle of Man. He studied at the Douglas School of Art and was a pupil teacher at St Barnabas Elementary School from 1878–1883. He taught at Douglas School of Art from 1884–1888, gaining his Art Master's Certificate in December 1889, and a

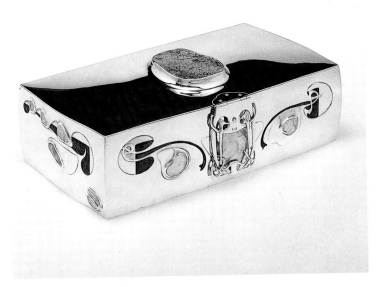

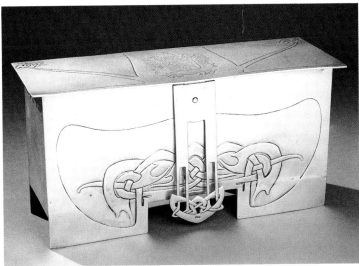

Above: *A jewel box by Archibald Knox in 'Cymric' silver, decorated with mother-of-pearl, enamel and turquoise. 28 cm (11¼ in.) wide. 1900*

Below: *A 'Cymric' silver scroll box by Archibald Knox with an interwoven Celtic pattern on the front. 25 cm (10 in.) wide. 1904*

Above: Silver and enamel chamberstick. Designed by Archibald Knox, 1903

period of designing for Liberty & Co. was from 1904–1906, when he supplied numerous designs for silver, pewter, jewellery, pottery and textiles. His last design for Liberty & Co. was for the memorial stone erected in memory of Arthur Lasenby Liberty at The Lee Church in Bucks in 1917. Most of his life, apart from designing for Liberty's, was spent in teaching and painting, dividing his time between the Isle of Man and England, with a brief spell in the United States in 1913. He died in 1933.

There is a great deal of variety in his designs, for tea and coffee services, boxes, candlesticks, cake trays, tankards, vases and clocks both in silver and pewter, and also silver mountings for glass claret jugs. All his designs are elegant, with a sensitive regard for both the material and function of the object, and are characterized by the use of entrelacs and other interlaced Celtic ornament and stylized plant forms, and spade and heart shapes. Another characteristic is the use of an extended thumbpiece to facilitate the lifting of the lid on tankards and jugs. Many of his pieces were decorated with enamels, predominantly in blue or green, or set with turquoise and blister pearls.

It seems unlikely that Knox produced any new designs after 1911, but some of his earlier designs continued to be produced, even in the 1920s. His role of principal designer passed to Harry

medal for historic ornament, specializing in Celtic Art, in 1892. For the next four years, he probably worked part-time in the offices of the architect M.H. Baillie Scott, but left the Isle of Man for London in 1897, obtaining a teaching post at Redhill in Surrey. It is thought that he may also have worked for, or had some connection with, Christopher Dresser as well as the Silver Studio.

His first involvement with Liberty & Co., in 1899, was probably through Baillie Scott, who had designed textiles for the firm from 1893. He was then commissioned to produce designs for 'Cymric' silver and, from 1901, designs for 'Tudric' pewter. His most prolific

Opposite: A 'Cymric' silver clock with copper numerals. Designed by Archibald Knox, c. 1903

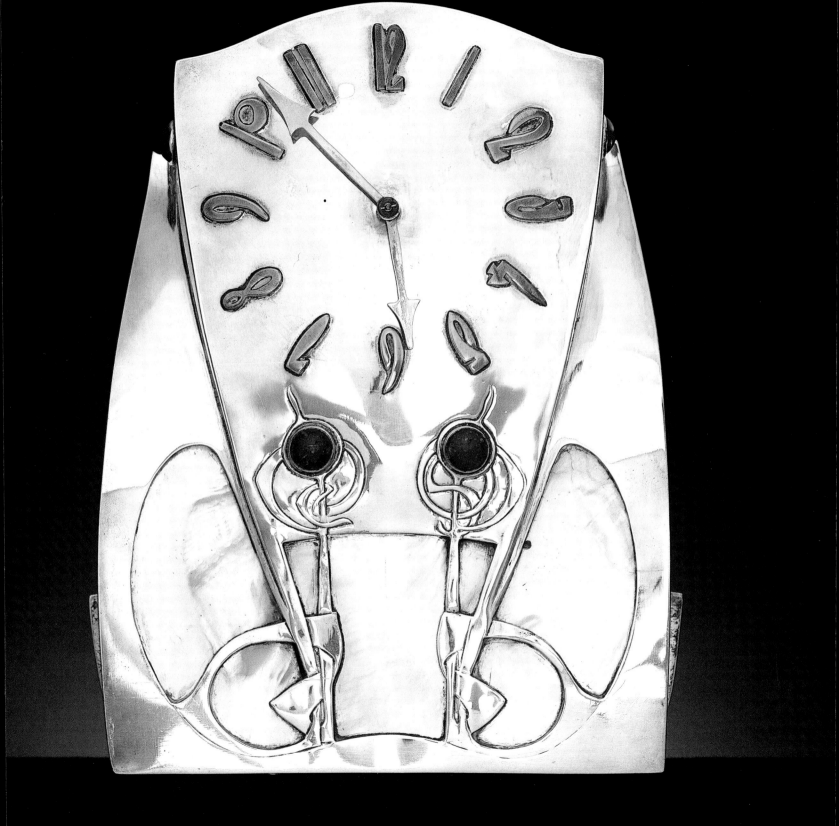

Craythorn, who worked for Haselers and was responsible for the design of a waist clasp of 1902. From 1910 to 1911 he was Haselers' chief designer and also one of the most skilled chasers to work for the firm.

Jessie Marion King

Another designer whose work is eagerly sought is Jessie Marion King (1876–1949), who was trained at the Glasgow School of Art, winning a travelling scholarship to Germany and Italy. A close friend of Charles Rennie Mackintosh, she worked in a delicate version of the Glasgow style, specializing in watercolours and book illustrations, which were strongly influenced by Aubrey Beardsley, but without the decadence and eroticism of his work. She won a gold medal for watercolours at the Turin Exhibition of 1902 and at this period also designed tiles, textiles, wallpapers, jewellery and silver, including designs for Liberty's. Her designs are more delicate, and more feminine, than those of Knox, and are usually adorned with tiny roses and other flowers, enamelled in blue. Typical of her work was a toilet set, consisting of powder box, clothes brush, hair brush and hand mirror, and a tortoiseshell comb, all with silver mounts with embossed swags of leaves and flowers enamelled in blue and green. Apart from the maker's mark of L & CO., the pieces are stamped Rd. 479297 indicating that the design was registered in 1906. The design has certain affinities with the 'Bara Ware' designs of William Moorcroft of approximately the same date, which had small pink roses on a cream ground, and were also used for toilet sets. Jessie King also designed a considerable number of belt and cloak clasps, including examples with enamelled flowers and birds on trellis work, and also pendants and brooches in a similar style. The hair brush and a delicate necklace are illustrated in *The Studio Year Book of Decorative Art* for 1909 (p. 143).

After 1906, most of the Silver Studio designs for Liberty silver and pewter seem to have been by Harry Silver (1882–1972), Rex's younger brother. While some of Harry Silver's designs show the influence of Knox, with interlaced Celtic motifs, others are 'Neo-Georgian', or have enamelled checked borders, recalling the work of Charles Rennie Mackintosh or the Wiener Werkstätte.

The enamelling on the 'Cymric' silver was normally confined to the high-lighting of individual motifs but, by about 1906, more pictorial enamelling began to appear, including a silver bowl, with a broad enamelled band with figures in a landscape, illustrated in *The Studio Year Book of Decorative Art* of 1906 (p. 240). Particularly attractive were the romantic, misty landscape panels by Fleetwood Charles Varley which were set into the lids of both silver and pewter boxes, or framed in oak as pictures. Fleetwood Charles Varley, a Chelsea watercolour artist, joined C.R.

Opposite: *Two enamelled plaques by Fleetwood Charles Varley, c. 1908*

Ashbee's Guild of Handicraft in 1899 or 1900, but left the Guild at Christmas 1907 shortly before its demise. An album of his designs for enamel work and jewellery is now in the Victoria & Albert Museum.

The catalogue of the first exhibition of 'Cymric' silver rightly stated that the early designs wre executed by hand but, as Maxwell Haseler (who was interviewed by both Shirley Bury and Mervyn Levy) stated, as the market grew it became too expensive to continue to make all the 'Cymric' silver entirely by hand. Machinery, such as spinning lathes, small hand-operated presses and foot-operated drop stamps, began to be used. Great care was taken not to alter the design in any way, and although cylindrical articles would be spun, the decoration would be chased, embossed, or incised by hand. Small articles such as the waist clasps and buckles, tea and coffee spoons and caddy spoons and buttons, which sold in considerable quantities, would be die-stamped. Openwork, however, would be pierced by hand-saw.

Pewter

As well as what they described as 'Reproductions of Mediaeval Pewter Ware', in 1898 (the year before the 'Cymric' silver and jewellery was launched), Liberty began to import modern German pewter, described in their catalogues as 'Novelties in Pewter Ware'. This German pewter, made mainly by J.P. Kayser and Sons of Krefeld, Walter Scherf and Co. of Nuremberg, and L. Lichtinger of Mu-

nich, was in the continental style of art nouveau and included candlesticks, jugs, goblets, bowls, and mounts for glass liqueur sets and decorative objects in Lötz glass. Considerably cheaper than the 'Cymric' silver, it had a ready sale, which no doubt influenced the decision to embark on a range of English pewter made by W.H. Haseler under the name of 'Tudric', which, like 'Cymric', owed its origin to John Llewellyn's Welsh ancestry.

Below: A 'Tudric' pewter clock, c. 1903

Above: *A 'Cymric' silver tea-set decorated with stylized Celtic knots. Designed by Archibald Knox. 1903*

A few designs were available by November 1901, and were mentioned in an article in the *Queen* magazine (vol. CX, 1901, p. 894) but the 'Tudric' pewter does not appear in the Liberty catalogues until 1902.

The fullest account of the venture is given in a paper on 'Pewter and the Revival of its Use', given to the Society of Arts by Arthur Lasenby Liberty on 17 May 1904 and printed in the *Society of Arts Journal* (vol. LII, 1904, pp. 626 *et seq.*) After a brief historical survey, Liberty went on to describe the differences between modern German and English pewter:

Modern German pewter, as compared to modern English, contains a much larger proportion of antimony, with some bismuth, and gives out when bent or bitten . . . the well-known crackle or cri . . . The German alloys have, however, in my opinion, the disadvantage of being more brittle than those used in this country and I refer particularly to those by the Company with which my own name is associated. The alloys used by it are, as before mentioned, the results of careful trials made by my friend, Mr Haseler, a Partner in, and Director of Liberty & Co.'s works at Birmingham. His endeavour has been to produce a metal similar, as far as possible, to the best of old English pewter and in point of solidity, the new alloy is, I believe, unequalled.

The actual composition was 90 per cent tin, 8 per cent copper, and 2 per cent antimony.

Having adopted the Celtic motif for silver and jewellery, the question arose, 'Why not apply the like forms and designs to the manufacture of pewter?'. Liberty went on to say that for pewter only modifications of Celtic forms were used, and these were soon supplemented by floral forms.

A number of German pieces were illustrated in the article, including a cake or fruit basket with aquatic ornament, a biscuit box with indentation on top of the handles making for easy gripping, a photograph frame, and a liqueur set and tray with floral ornament in low relief.

As with the Cymric silver, the Knox designs were probably the most successful, and several were illustrated in the article. However, the designs tended to be simpler and more austere than those for silver. Tripod bowls, and circular stands with ear-like handles, were made to hold glass dishes, as well as holders for glass butter dishes. The glass was usually a green bottle glass and was made by James Powell & Sons of Whitefriars, who also supplied the glass for the silver-mounted claret jugs.

One of the most popular pewter items was a biscuit box designed by Knox about 1903. The cube form had slightly lobed sides, and was decorated with three horizontal bands of stylized square-shaped flowers and leaves. It was made for a number of years and as late as 1924 was copied for the firm of Carr & Co. of Carlisle, by N.C. Joseph Ltd. of Stratford-on-Avon. Called the 'ART BOX' it was described in Carr's 1924 brochure as 'A most artistic Biscuit Box in aluminium. The chaste design and rich effect of this box cannot but add great refinement to the table'. Visually, the only alteration was a flat circular disc on the top of the lid instead of the two curved handles in the centre of the original. Whether this was a blatant case of plagiarism, or whether it was done with Liberty's approval is not known.

Unlike the 'Cymric' silver, the pewter which was produced in larger quantities was never executed by hand, but was made in iron moulds. For cheaper articles it would have been too expensive to produce the raised motifs by hand (particularly the complicated interlaced designs of Archibald Knox), but great care was taken to produce fine casts unblemished by any bubbles.

Unfortunately, during 1909–1910, Liberty's sold a number of Knox's designs to Connell and Company of Cheapside, who produced their own range of pewter, which was inferior to that made by Haseler for Liberty.

Jewellery

Before Liberty introduced their own range of silver and gold jewellery in an 'arts and crafts' style, they sold an incredible variety of inexpensive jewellery from both the Near and Far East, and from Europe, much of which can best be described as 'peasant' or 'reproduction' jewellery. Representative examples are illustrated in the 1888 *Yuletide Gifts* catalogue of 'Art Novelties for Personal Attire and Home Adornment'.

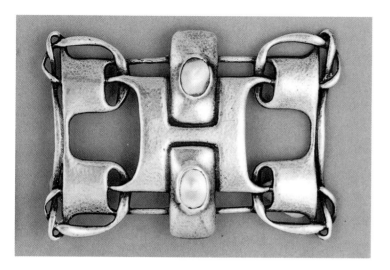

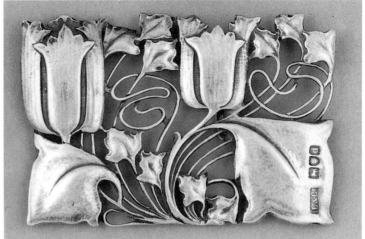

Reproductions of old Flemish jewellery included silver clasps and waist buckles, chatelaines and brooches in Renaissance and Rococo designs with elaborate scrolls and figures of cherubs or *putti*. Reproductions of 'Greek' and 'Etruscan' jewellery, and what was described as 'Renaissance' jewellery, were produced in oxydized silver, while from Damascus came silver filigree necklaces, bracelets, brooches and belt buckles.

The Far Eastern merchandise included Japanese chain bracelets composed of inlaid metal beads in the form of miniature vases and figures, moonstone jewellery from Ceylon, and iridescent shell necklaces from Fiji. More expensive Eastern jewellery, set with precious and semiprecious stones was also available, together with Indian, Chinese and Japanese gold necklets. Similar items of imported jewellery were sold throughout the 1890s, but late in 1898 or early in 1899, Liberty turned his attention to sponsoring a range of original jewellery which fea-

tured in the May 1899 exhibition of 'Cymric' silver. This included a number of silver buckles and clasps, mostly in Celtic style, and like the silver, given archaic-sounding names such as 'Cedric', 'Exon', 'Scyld', 'Runic' and 'Mercia'. A number of gold brooches were also included. The Silver Studio collection includes three designs in pencil and watercolour for silver brooches, inscribed 'The Leoc', 'The Lingan' and 'The Abban', all of which have the complex interlaced Celtic patterns of Archibald Knox, and the actual brooches are illustrated in Liberty's *Cymric Silver* catalogue of 1899 or 1900.

Above: *Two silver buckles, the left one possibly designed by Knox, the right by the Silver Studio.*

Overleaf left: *A diamond and moonstone pendant designed by Archibald Knox*

Overleaf right: *A Liberty necklace in gold, opal and pearl, c. 1905*

The 1905 Liberty catalogue of *Jewellery & Silverware* described the items as being in:

> . . . *new designs on the lines of ancient types aiming at freedom from mechanical restraint and monotony in treatment* . . .
>
> *The stock in the showrooms is practically a fine art exhibition on a small scale showing the most recent developments in the Jewellers' and Silversmiths' craft. The goods are marked in plain figures and the assistants are instructed not to solicit visitors to make purchases.*

Above: *A gold brooch set with pearls and opals, with its original case. 1905*

Anyone browsing among the exhibits would have found a great variety of jewellery catering for widely different tastes and pockets. The silver brooches included interlaced Celtic designs by Knox, set with turquoise and pearls or decorated with enamels, others with typical art nouveau designs of stylized tulips, flattened heart shapes, and heart-shaped leaves on meandering stalks. The gold brooches, some set with gems, some of them by Knox, were on the whole more conventional, and there were also pendants in a more typical Edwardian style with bows and flowers in pearl and marcasite, catering for more conservative tastes.

Very characteristic were necklaces with shaped units in gold or silver, linked with gold or silver chains, often with a larger centre pendant. These were typical of the 'arts and crafts' jewellery of the time, and were often set with moonstones, baroque or blister pearls, or decorated with enamels. Although jewellery continued to be made by Haseler's, and bore the Liberty and Haseler marks, a number of the pieces appear to have been made in Pforzheim through the agency of Murlle Bennett & Co., an Anglo-German concern, with premises in Charterhouse Street. Some of the pieces of jewellery that appears in both Liberty and Haseler catalogues were advertised by Murlle Bennett as their own productions.

A bleached horn tiara, in the form of ears of corn, with details carved and stained on the back, mounted with moonstones in a claw setting and fixed on a metal band, was accompanied by its original box labelled LIBERTY & CO/ REGENT STREET/LONDON, and was shown in the Centenary Exhibition of 1975. It dates from about 1905 and although it shows the influence of French art nouveau jewellery, it was almost certainly made by Fred Partridge who, like Pearson and Varley, had worked for the Guild of Handicraft. A similar piece of horn jewellery by Fred Partridge is now in the Cheltenham Museum and Art Gallery.

The 1907 *Yule-Tide Gifts* catalogue shows some of the earlier Celtic style designs of jewellery – brooches, buckles, clasps and hatpins – but more conventional designs predominate, and the designs, in both silver and pewter, tend to be simpler and plainer, together with German pewter in rather austere 'Jugendstil' designs.

There is little doubt that the Celtic designs of Knox and the Silver Studios, together with the art nouveau textiles, were instrumental in promoting the Liberty style, both at home and abroad. The success of the Cymric silver and jewellery and, to a lesser extent the pewter, contributed to the collapse of Ashbee's Guild of Handicraft, for to the public at least here was a similar range of goods, catering for the same artistic tastes but at a fraction of the cost. Ashbee himself was quite vitriolic about Liberty's. In *Craftsmanship in Competitive Industry* (1908), he called it the great house of Novelty, Nobody & Co., 'who have done me the honour of stealing silverwork from me . . . [producing] mechanical or underpaid imitations in some phthisical (sic) cubby hole in a black, back street in the model City of Birmingham'; and his wife Janet was equally bitter. Admittedly, some of the pieces by the Guild of Handicraft undoubtedly excel those of Liberty's, but the criticism is somewhat unfair, as Liberty's were no mere plagiarists. Although some of the designs were influenced by the Guild's work, most of the Liberty designs were entirely original, and many of them, particularly in the early days, were equally well made.

'The Studio' by Leonard Wyburd

98

Chapter Five

FURNITURE AND INTERIOR DECORATION

Little furniture, other than small Oriental items, was available before 1883, when a Furnishing and Decoration Studio was set up under the direction of the designer, Leonard F. Wyburd, who was to be associated with Liberty's for more than twenty years. His own speciality was the Moorish or 'Mushrebiyeh' style, but the Studio was nothing if not eclectic and it produced furniture in a wide range of designs from Tudor and Jacobean to Flemish, German Gothic and English eighteenth century country style. The most characteristic Liberty furniture was sturdily constructed in oak, with elaborate metal fittings, and frequently embellished with an appropriate motto.

There is a considerable variety in the furniture and styles of interior decoration produced by Liberty's between 1880 and 1910. On 13 March 1900, Arthur Lasenby Liberty gave a lecture on *English Furniture* to the Society of Arts (*Society of Arts Journal*, vol. XLVIII, p. 369 *et seq.*). He began his talk with a brief historical survey in which he stated that our finest period of furniture began with the accession of James I, declined during the first half of the 19th century until the 'Gothic revival brought us back to first principles of construction and directness of design'. He went on to stress the importance of comfort — 'Better a Windsor chair with comfort than a *chaise à la Louis Quinze* which makes

Above: *Saracenic Smoking Room, from* Liberty's Handbook of Sketches, *n.d.*

one's back ache' — also stating that 'Utility, which means fitness, is in itself beauty if rightly understood'. Certainly, apart from some of the Oriental imports, most Liberty furniture was well made and soundly constructed, but not all of it can be said to measure up to his other dictum of 'no unnecessary decoration'.

'Anglo-Oriental' furniture

As Godwin had stated in 1876 (*The Architect*, 23 December), for the first year there was no 'decent furniture', but early in 1880 Liberty's decided to departmentalize their stock, furniture being sold by the 'D' Department. The catalogue of oriental goods, *Eastern Art Manufactures and Decorative Objects*, published in 1881, included a section labelled 'Department D', with carved wooden pieces from China and Japan, together with cane chairs, stools and wastepaper baskets from North Africa. Apart from these imported goods, small items of bamboo furniture such as overmantels and shelves were described as 'Anglo-Oriental'. The catalogue also offered to have 'Special designs made to order – drawings post free'. This Anglo-Oriental furniture was made by a French craftsman, Monsieur Ursin Fortier, originally a basket maker, who had premises in Soho. Liberty's placed their first order with M. Fortier in 1881 and he continued to work exclusively for Liberty's throughout the 1880s, supplying a variety of bamboo furniture including chairs and tables, cabinets and writing desks inset with panels of Japanese lacquer, leather paper or 'old gold' matting, and smaller items such as hanging shelves, easels and cakestands. In the 1890s the bamboo furniture was called 'Anglo-Indian' or 'Chinese' and the range widened to include chairs and settees upholstered in 'Djijim Kelims'.

As well as being available in the Regent Street shop, some of the early Liberty furniture was shown in the galleries of the Royal School of Needlework in South Kensington. In 1883 *The Cabinet Maker and Art Furnisher* (vol. III, 1883, p. 182) included Liberty's among its list of high class firms selling furniture, stating that:

Above: *The four-legged 'Thebes' stool, usually made in walnut*

. . . *some of the cane chairs, carved cabinets, screens and flower stands shown by this enterprising firm are marvels of art and cheapness. Messrs. Liberty are evidently educating their Oriental producers as to the wants of our market and the result is that an English home can be almost entirely furnished with Eastern goods'.*

Such furniture, however, would have had a limited appeal, and it became obvious that a wider range should be available. Accordingly, in 1883 Liberty's set up a Furnishing and Decoration Studio under the direction of Leonard Wyburd, a painter who exhibited at the Royal Academy from 1888 to 1905, describing himself as 'Painter and Architect'. Wyburd retired from Liberty's in 1903 but continued to work independently describing himself, in an advertisement in the *Studio Year Book* of 1906, as 'Designer and expert adviser in Decorations and Furniture – over 20 years with Liberty & Co.'

A wide variety of furniture in a number of different styles was to be produced by, or for, the Liberty Furniture and Decoration Studio under his direction, but Wyburd's own speciality was 'Moorish' furniture and decoration, or Egyptian based designs.

The Thebes stools

Among the earliest items of furniture that can be fully documented were two stools, based on ancient Egyptian prototypes, both called the 'Thebes' and registered in 1884. One, a four-legged stool, usually made in walnut but also in mahogany, with turning on the lower legs and a leather seat attached to the frame with thonging, has the Patent Office Design registration No. 16673. It was hardly an original design, as the ancient Egyptian prototype had already inspired a number of artists and designers earlier in the century. A drawing of a similar Egyptian stool by J.G. Grace, dated 1853, is now in the RIBA, and Ford Madox Brown designed a comparable Egyptian style chair for Holman Hunt in 1857. A number of other artists, including Christopher Dresser and E.W. Godwin, produced drawings of ancient Egyptian furniture in the 1870s. It is tempting to suggest that

Godwin, who was then in charge of Liberty's Costume Studio, may have had a hand in the origin of this 'Thebes' stool, for a drawing of the prototype occurs on a page of museum studies in a Godwin sketchbook of about 1875. The stool was to prove immensely popular and was produced over a number of years. One can be seen in a contemporary photograph of Arthur Lasenby Liberty's drawing room at The Lee Manor, the house he lived in from 1892.

The other 'Thebes' stool had three curved legs fixed directly into the dished seat which was carved from a solid piece of wood. It was made both in oak and mahogany, sometimes stained or lacquered red, and bears the registered number 16674. It was to prove equally popular, appearing in the firm's catalogues certainly as late as 1907. It was sold by Samuel Bing when he opened his shop, La Maison de l'Art Nouveau, in Paris in November 1895 and in a number of other retail outlets in Europe, finding its way into museum collections as far afield as the Nordenfjeldske Kunstindustrimuseum in Trondheim, Norway, which purchased one from Bing in 1896.

It was copied by the Austrian architect Adolf Loos (1870–1933), who claimed it as his own design, and also stained it red. He also stained red the bentwood chairs, made by Kohn, that he designed for the Café Museum in Vienna in 1899.

Leonard Wyburd

Leonard Wyburd's real speciality in the early days of the Furniture & Decora-

The second 'Thebes' stool had three legs fixed directly into its dished seat. The paper label from the underside of this stool is reproduced on page 99

tion Studio was the 'Moorish' style which he employed not only for smoking rooms, but also for drawing rooms, and Liberty's own 'Arab' tea rooms. He was not the first in the field, for Owen Jones (1809–1874) had already executed Moorish designs for furniture and interiors earlier in the century, and the firm of H. & J. Cooper of Great Pulteney Street were known for their Arabian and Moorish interiors from about 1875.

Liberty's owned a copy of *Les Arts Arabes* by Jules Bourgoin, published in 1867, which as Viollet-le-Duc stated in the preface, was 'a practical and complete treatise which reveals a whole new order of composition'. This, no doubt, provided an important source of inspiration for Wyburd. At first he seems mainly to have relied on imported furniture from North Africa, including inlaid coffee tables, Kharan stands, screens etc., but he soon began to design

Below: Two armchairs from a Liberty Moorish oak suite with panels of Mushrebiyeh lattice-work, designed by Leonard Wyburd, c. 1884

original 'Moorish' furniture, often incorporating panels of *Mushrebiyeh* lattice-work. J. Moyr Smith in his book, *Ornamental Interiors, Ancient and Modern* (1887), reported that Liberty's:

> . . . *showed a variety of art furniture in the Moorish or Arab style, most of it being light and elegant in form and moderate in price. The importation of Mushrebiyeh lattice-work from Egypt has probably induced Messrs. Liberty & Co. to turn this exceedingly artistic material to practical account; they have accordingly in their Kharan chairs made very tasteful use of this fascinating artistic product of Mohammedan Egypt, and in Arabic cabinets, Mushrebiyeh screens, camphor or sandalwood tables, punkahs, traciered lamps, and Arabic stained glass windows of beautiful flowing designs and splendid colour are used to produce an Oriental effect.*

Moyr Smith illustrated a Moorish smoking room as well as an occasional table and rush-seated chair incorporating *Mushrebiyeh* panels.

A tribute to the quality of Liberty's Moorish style is given in *The Cabinet Maker and Art Furnisher* for 1 April 1884 (p. 184). Having described the Moorish style of Messrs. Cooper, the writer stated that:

> *Messrs. Liberty & Co. . . . have fitted up apartments quite in the same style as the foregoing, and, from a commercial point of view, their display is more practical, because their*

'*adaptation of Arabian Art*' — *as they define it* — *is really consistent with inexpensive furnishing. They have applied the style, more or less successfully, to various cheap forms of ordinary furniture.*

The accompanying illustration showed three Anglo-Moresque chairs. The wooden armchair in the centre, which had panels of *musharabeyeh* (sic), was stained darkish green and was said to be 'remarkably easy and not uncomely' when made comfortable by the addition of a few cushions. An example of this chair is now in the Cecil Higgins Museum, Bedford. The chair on the left was described as a good model, and the bracket supports to the legs and back were praised as good, constructive features, giving strength to an otherwise rather flimsy design. The third chair, like some of the Thebes stools, was painted vermilion red, and had a Moorish arch motif cut out of the back, and splayed straight legs. It was described as a 'crude looking chair' which 'is an example of that vermilion coloured furniture which has been of late, so much in demand. When there are

Overleaf left: *A Moorish style occasional table in walnut stamped* 'Liberty & Co. 513. Height 65 cm (25½ in.), c. 1885

Overleaf right: *A walnut table from Liberty's, similar to those designed by E.W. Godwin, c. 1885. Height 73 cm (28¾ in.)*

two or three pieces in a room, the effect is, I think too florid; but a single piece frequently helps to light up an apartment'. The furniture was displayed in a room with Egyptian red walls, the ceiling painted in colours with a Saracenic design; some of the *Mushrebiyeh* screening had coloured glass behind it, and lamps hung from the ceiling. There were also folding stands for brass trays, brackets, what-nots, and fabrics. The writer pointed out how Liberty's were not content to act merely as importers, but:

> . . . *wisely perceive that a much larger trade can be secured if the public are only shown how the treasures and styles of the East can be transformed or utilised for the purpose of everyday life in this country. Thus they embrace in their present business home-made productions in the Moresque style, as well as originals, and the clever way in which the two are wedded does considerable credit to the firm. I have never seen a display of such goods more calculated to secure business or to meet the wants of middle class as well as wealthy buyers.*

The Moorish style was to feature prominently in Liberty catalogues and sketches of interior decoration well into the next century, for their *Three Styles of Furniture and Decoration*, published in 1909, features an 'Eastern smoking room'. Indian elements were often mixed with the Arab style and a number of the interiors were designated merely as 'Oriental'. *The Liberty Hand-book of Sketches with Prices and Other Information for Artistic and Economical Domestic Decoration and Furniture*, which has been tentatively dated 1889 although it is probably slightly later, shows folding *Mushrebiyeh* lattice screens, Kharan chairs and writing table, an Anglo-Arab drawing room, a section of an Arab hall, and a morning room in Arab style. It also includes a press report of 13 April 1889, under the heading 'An Eastern Dream' which describes the Eastern Music Room and corridor at 27 Grosvenor Square, which was executed for Lady Aberdeen, the wife of the 7th Earl and 1st Marquess of Aberdeen. The room was described as:

> . . . *a triumph of taste and a monument to 'Liberty' enterprise and art. The ceiling panels are modelled from windows around the tombs of the Queens of Shah-Ahmed at Ahmedabad, the leaded glass from the designs of the tombs of Yufus Mooltan; the exquisite lattices hail from the Punjab, the fire dogs from Nepal, and the tiles from Mooltan. Pure and perfect Orientalism are supreme in this exquisite room.*

Wide variety of styles

As in this *Handbook of Sketches*, together with other Liberty publications of the late 1880s and 1890s, eclecticism was rife, with orientalism going hand-in-hand with revived English styles, which

Opposite: *The Windsor-style beech armchair featured in the* Yule-tide Gifts *catalogue of 1895–6 and sold in Europe*

ranged from Tudor and Jacobean to 18th century country furniture, and catered for a wide range of artistic tastes. Liberty's emulated Morris and Company in producing a considerable variety of rush-seated chairs with the names 'Chesham', 'Wykeham', 'Hampden', 'Argyle' and 'Arundel'. The 'Lincoln' set, which had turned decoration recalling some of the simulated bamboo furniture of the Regency period, comprised a settee, a gentleman's chair, a lady's chair and six single chairs, all for the price of 10 guineas. The 'Lincoln' child's chair could be bought separately for 7/6d in the ebonised version, or for 10/6d in walnut. The 'Norfolk' was a corner chair composed of ebonised bobbin turning; and a three-legged stool with a round seat called the 'Patience' was advertised as being in 'Art Colours'. These adaptations of English country furniture, introduced in the 1880s and 1890s, sold well into the 20th century. A simple Windsor-like chair, made in beech and stained green, which appears in the Liberty *Yule-Tide Gifts* catalogue of 1895–6 was certainly sold abroad, for one was purchased by the Nordenfjeldske Kunstindustrimuseum in Trondheim from Messrs Hirschwald of Berlin in 1902. Most of this type of furniture would have been made by outside firms, including William Birch of High Wycombe, but how much of it was exclusive to Liberty's is not clear. The Liberty *Yule-Tide Gifts* catalogue of 1892 illustrates a chair with five spokes converging from the shaped top towards the upholstered seat, which is set on four splayed legs and is described as the

'Antwerpen' chair, 'A quaint chair, strong and light, made of walnut, seat upholstered and covered with tapestry. Price 15/-'. The identical chair, however, was illustrated in the *Cabinet Maker and Art Furnisher* (1 January 1889, p. 172) described as an 'old fashioned type of kitchen chair refined up to the form of a "gossip" chair painted in artistic green, with a prettily upholstered seat', and was sold by Messrs Hindley & Sons, who specialized in reproductions of 18th century English furniture.

Oak furniture

The most characteristic Liberty furniture was made in oak, solidly and well constructed in a somewhat rugged style, partly based on English rural forms. It was often embellished with beaten copper plaques, elaborate copper hinges, lock plates and handles, and with leaded glass cupboard doors, and sometimes an appropriate carved inscription at the top. A typical example of this style is a huge oak sideboard with copper fittings, including a repoussé copper panel of two ships and a flying dragon, which is flanked by two small cupboards with leaded glass panels. At the top is the rather curious carved inscription 'IT IS THE FAIR ACCEPTANCE THAT CREATES THE ENTERTAINMENT NOT THE CATES' (cates being purchased provisions, as opposed to homemade ones). Below are two cupboards with copper hinges, escutcheons and drop handles. The sideboard was designed by Leonard Wyburd and was illustrated in the *Studio* (vol. II, 1894, p. 35) and also later in the *House* (vol. I, 1897, p. 90). An earlier, simpler example was a rather 'mediaeval' sideboard with heavy hinges and locks that was illustrated by Moyr Smith in 1887, citing it as an example 'of a very simple and inexpensive style of dining room furniture which yet had spirit and individuality'. To emphasize the 'mediaeval' quality, the sideboard was set with German stoneware and *roemers*, and reproductions of old Venetian glass.

By the 1890s a considerable range of this heavy oak furniture, including sideboards, bookcases, tables, chairs and bedroom suites, was available, much of it designed by Wyburd himself. Most were given 'Saxon' or Scottish names and the oak was 'rendered the colour and finish of old work'. A characteristic example, one of several variants, was the 'Lochleven Buffet', introduced about 1890, which had a small cupboard, glazed with leaded 'bulls-eyes', and two open compartments on a shelf raised from the board by turned columns, with a drawer and cupboards below. Such items sold abroad as well as at home, and a 'Lochleven Buffet' was purchased by the Osterreichisches Museum für angewandte Kunst in Vienna. A very similar bookcase, with the same kind of assymetrical arrangement of open shelves and a glazed cupboard above a fall-front desk had a carved inscription at the top 'READING MAKYTH A FULL MAN WRITING AN EXACT MAN'. In somewhat similar style but lighter, were shelves for bric-à-brac, a combined clock and wall bracket called 'The Thoecen', and the 'Raleigh' smoker's cabinet with the dubious motto 'THE MAN WHO SMOKES THINKS LIKE A SAGE AND ACTS LIKE A SAMARITAN'. These and other similar articles appear in the *Yule-Tide Gifts* catalogue of 1895–6.

The 'Culloden' suite had a sideboard made in finely grained oak, enriched with wrought copper fittings, with an upper cupboard glazed with leaded glass, and drawers and lockers below. The accompanying rush-seated dining chairs, with broad slatted backs, were similar to those produced by Morris & Company in the 1890s. A *Yule-Tide Gifts* catalogue, undated, but probably 1899, includes a two page central section

Below: *The 'Lochleven' oak sideboard with a leaded glass cupboard door and hammered iron fittings, probably designed by Leonard Wyburd*

illustrating a number of smaller pieces of furniture including the 'Wiclif' chair 'of quaint and simple design', and two heavy rush-seated armchairs, the 'Ethelbert' and the 'Athelstan'. The Athelstan design featured as a bedroom suite in the Liberty *Furniture* catalogue of 1902, described as a serviceable and artistic suite in solid oak. The upper panel of the door of the wardrobe had a hand-stained panel of a landscape, and

Opposite: *'The Athelstan' wardrobe, featured in Liberty's* Furniture *catalogue of 1902*

Below: *A Liberty oak wardrobe from a bedroom suite, c. 1900*

heart-shaped cut-outs, the latter a feature of many Liberty pieces around the turn of the century. The washstand had 'antique' tiles at the top and back and the dressing table had rather primitive looking handles made of a piece of oak dowelling attached to the drawers by small rectangles of wood at either end. The same handles appeared on another bedroom suite by Leonard Wyburd of about 1899 which showed an Egyptian influence, being embellished with 'Lotus' insets in pewter, and a lotus design stencilled on the matting splashback of the washstand which was attached to the frame by thonging.

Wyburd also produced a number of smaller items such as the 'Sigebert' table; this had a hexagonal top and art nouveau tulip motifs cut out of the three legs, which were joined by three stretchers forming a triangle. Art nouveau fretwork also adorned the 'Suffolke' stand, which combined an occasional table with shelves for books or objects.

It is difficult to ascertain to what extent these designs of the 1890s were by Wyburd himself. An undated *Handbook of Sketches, Part II, Reception Rooms, Halls, Dining Rooms, Drawing Rooms, Boudoirs, Morning Rooms, Smoking Rooms and Billiard Rooms* probably spans dates from 1893 to 1900, for the first sketch, 'A Summer Cottage' is signed by V.T. Jones and dated 1893, whereas other sketches labelled 'Recent developments' are manifestly later. The sketches include 'The Witlaf' sideboard, in solid oak, with an embossed copper panel of boys in a Viking

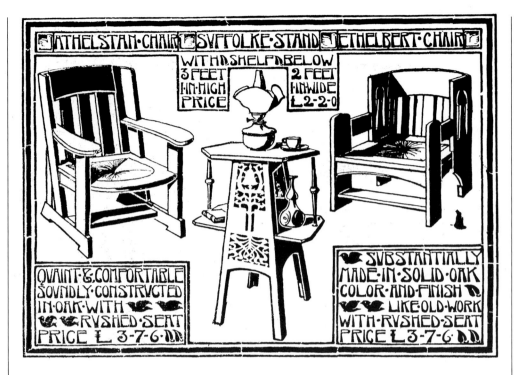

ship, which is signed H.F.T; other illustrations, including a Dutch breakfast room with a frieze of 'Old World Battleships' above the dado, are signed P.E.Q. in monogram, while a Saracenic smoking room design is signed G. Hentschel. These unidentified initials are possibly those of the studio draughtsmen, rather than the designers, for an illustration of a morning room called the 'Rossetti' (as it included reproductions of his paintings) shows the 'Sigebert' table and the 'Suffolke' stand, both of which have been attributed to Wyburd. Little is known of the personnel of the Furnishing and Decoration Studio, apart from E.P. Roberts who joined the design team in 1887, and succeeded to the management in 1903 on Wyburd's retirement. According to the *Liberty Lamp* (vol. VI, 1930, p. 126), Liberty's first took over a workshop of

their own in 1887. It was supervised by a Scot, James Thallon, who had as his foreman George Wolfe, who had previously worked with Thallon at the cabinet-works of Messrs Howard of Berners Street. When James Thallon retired in 1898, his son took over, to be succeeded in turn by George Wolfe who remained with the firm until his retirement in 1931. Not all the furniture was produced in the Liberty workshops, some probably being made by independent craftsmen. Certainly, both chairs and cabinet furniture were made for Liberty's by William Birch of High Wycombe, some of it designed by

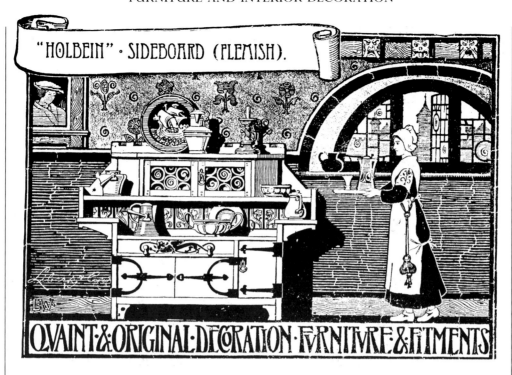

"HOLBEIN" · SIDEBOARD (FLEMISH).

QVAINT·&·ORIGINAL·DECORATION·FVRNITVRE·&·FITMENTS

E.G. Punnett. Punnett was possibly responsible for some of the more elegant pieces of Liberty furniture which were first produced in the late 1890s. This furniture was made in mahogany or walnut, or occasionally in satinwood, rather than in oak. It often shows the influence of C.F.A. Voysey and is similar to that produced by J.S. Henry of Old Street, a firm which also employed E.G. Punnett as a designer.

A typical Liberty piece is a music cabinet made in 1897 or 1898, which is now in the Bowes Museum, Barnard Castle. Made of mahogany, it has four capped posts rising above the main carcase, and art nouveau plant decoration in coloured woods on the doors and upper rails. The same style can be seen in an elegant mahogany display cabinet of approximately the same date, which has glazed doors, marquetry in coloured

Above: 'The Holbein' sideboard (Flemish)', an illustration from Liberty's Handbook of Sketches. *An illustration by Leonard Wyburd, 1894*

woods and mother-of-pearl, and elaborate brass lock plates and handles set with small blue ceramic bosses. A number of occasional tables have similar art nouveau floral marquetry. An equally elegant suite in walnut, inlaid with delicate motifs in mother-of-pearl, was designed by the Glasgow architect George Walton (1867–1933). George Walton, the son of an unsuccessful painter, after attending evening classes at Glasgow School of Art, abandoned his career as a bank clerk and set himself up as 'George Walton & Co., Ecclesiastical and House Decorators' in 1888. He moved to London in 1897, and

The mahogany music cabinet which was made in 1897 or 1898 and is now in the Bowes Museum, Barnard Castle, Co. Durham. It is described on page 115

in 1898 secured an important commission to furnish Kodak showrooms in London, Glasgow, Brussels, Milan and Vienna, and continued to pursue a successful career as an architect and designer of stained glass, furniture, textiles and wallpapers. As well as designing furniture, he also designed some of the later 'Clutha' glass sold by Liberty. A satinwood drawing room suite, with a glazed cabinet, two armchairs, single chairs and a table, virtually identical to one in a Liberty *Inexpensive Furniture* catalogue of about 1905, clearly shows the influence of George Walton although it may not have been designed by him. There is a strong 'Glasgow style' influence in much of the Liberty furniture of this date, as shown in the room settings in their *Dress and Decoration* publication of 1905. Wylie and Lochhead of Glasgow retailed some Liberty furniture and there is a distinct similarity between some of their pieces, particularly the hall furniture.

As well as their original styles, Liberty's was responsible for a number of revivals. Prominent among them was the so-called 'Jacobean' style, which Liberty described as 'perhaps the most ENGLISH in its characteristics . . . and in many respects the most suitable to our climate, tastes and habits'. This style was considered particularly suitable for halls, staircases, billiard rooms and dining rooms, with tables with bulbous carved legs, inglenooks and oak panelling, with plaster friezes and ceilings, some executed by G.F. Bankart. What was called 'Modified Tudor' or 'Domestic Gothic' also found favour, and often incorporated linenfold oak panelling which was to become a Liberty speciality. 'Elizabethan' and 'English Renaissance' are also found, and while English revivals predominated, an occasional foreign influence was permitted. The 'Holbein' sideboard designed by Wyburd, which has similar decoration to that on the shelves and brackets in the 1895–6 *Yule-Tide Gifts* catalogue, is described as 'Flemish', while the 'Culloden' dining room is described as 'German Gothic'. Unlike many of their competitors, Liberty did not favour French styles, and avoided the fashionable 'Neo-Rococo' and 'Louis Quinze' and 'Louis Seize' styles. These varied styles of Liberty interior decoration, perhaps because of their very Englishness, had a marked success abroad, and commissions were received throughout Europe and from as far afield as India and South Africa.

Apart from permanent schemes of interior decoration, Liberty's were also involved in more ephemeral and exotic schemes for exhibitions and other special occasions. As well as providing the materials for the costumes for F.C. Burnand's play *The Colonel*, adapted from a French play satirising the aesthetes, and the Gilbert and Sullivan opera *Patience*, when the latter transferred from the Opéra Comique to the newly built Savoy Theatre (designed by the architect Charles John Phipps (1835–1897)) which had opened on 14 October 1881, Liberty's designed a special reception room for the Prince of Wales, festooning the room with a selection of Liberty silks. Similar decorations were provided on occasions for the Royal Opera House, Covent Garden, the Haymarket Theatre, the Lyceum and Drury Lane. For *The Mikardo* (1885), with its Japanese setting one of the most popular of the Gilbert and Sullivan operas, Liberty sent representatives to Japan to study the native costumes at first hand, and bring back correct materials for both the costumes and stage sets.

Special schemes

In 1875 Arthur Liberty had been involved in setting up a Japanese house in the park at Alexandra Palace in North London, but in 1885 he was to undertake an even more ambitious project, the setting up of an Indian Village at the Albert Exhibition Palace in Battersea Park. This was a cast iron and glass building similar to the Crystal Palace and was first erected for an exhibition in Dublin, and then moved to Battersea in southwest London. This enterprise involved bringing over a whole contingent of native Indian craftsmen, entertainers, musicians and cooks. A Liberty employee, Mr A. Bonner, had the rather daunting task of collecting the Indians and bringing them to England, complicated by the fact that the Indians belonged to different castes and religions, including Hindu, Mohammedan, Zoroastrian and Roman Catholic. The craftsmen included spinners, weavers, dyers, dressmakers and embroiderers, brass workers and jewellers, carvers and inlaid woodworkers and modelmakers, and among the entertainers were a snake charmer, an acrobat, jugglers and dancing girls. The idea was to show the skill of the Indian craftsmen and no doubt also to promote Liberty's own Indian imports.

Liberty's also provided decorations for Queen Victoria's Golden Jubilee in 1887 and for the celebrations of the Silver Wedding of the Prince and Princess of Wales in the following year. Perhaps the most exotic of these ventures was the decoration of the Royal Pavilion at Brighton on the occasion of a ball given for a wealthy Indian Prince, the Maharaja Gaekwar of Baroda, who was spending the winter of 1887–8 in the town. Guy Bentley, writing many years later in the *Liberty Lamp* in 1927, recalled that:

. . . several truck loads of carpets, rugs, embroideries, palampores and other Oriental goods valued at over £2,000 were transported to Brighton, and in about forty-eight hours the Pavilion was transformed into a scene from the Arabian Nights.

Guy Bentley, with two other Liberty employees, attended the ball, and he described how 'the Rani (the Prince's wife) was concealed in a small room fitted up for her where, behind Musharabeyeh screens, she could watch the festivities'.

Opposite: *Oak mantel clock, the face inlaid with pewter, which was designed by C.F.A. Voysey and sold by Liberty's, c. 1900*

The Royal Pavilion transformed

The ball took place on 8 December and a full description of the decorations was given in the *Brighton Guardian* for 14 December 1887. Described as being 'decorated internally with the most lavish Oriental splendour', the Gaekwar's colours of yellow and dark blue were used throughout the scheme. In one apartment the colours were emphasized in the festooned hangings of Indian muslin and rich embroideries, and in the chief supper chambers they were again found most appropriately blended in the spread tail of a peacock, which formed a conspicuous table ornament. The doorway leading to the main corridor was decorated with a sumptuous piece of antique Chinese embroidery worked with figures in crimson and gold silks, with on either side Japanese panels embroidered with storks. The seating in the corridor was covered with Turkish and Persian rugs and the natural divisions of the apartment were adorned

Above: A dining room designed and executed by Liberty & Co., 1906. This watercolour is reproduced in the Studio Yearbook of Decorative Art, *1906*

overhead with festooned curtains of yellow Indian muslin. The walls were hung with Japanese embroideries, glittering with gold thread, and open fans of cerulean blue silk and yellow flowers added to the colour scheme. Large palm trees were set at intervals; the floor was covered with brightly coloured rugs, and mirrors reflected the splendour of the scheme. The double staircase at the north end of the corridor was hung with printed Indian palampores. The Saloon was furnished as a throne room and the dais, approached by two or three steps, was covered with a fine Dhurrie carpet, overarched with a canopy of blue and gold, with draperies at the back. The chair of honour, or throne, was in crimson velvet and gold with a tapestry behind embellished with the Gaekwar's

crest of a crown and a scimitar.

The two large apartments, the Music Room and Banqueting Room, were set aside for dancing, and the settees covered with Persian rugs. Platforms decorated with festoons of muslin were provided for the bands, and were surmounted by a frieze composed of Indian hand screens of *kus-kus* grass. The oblong chamber behind the Banqueting Room was transformed into a retiring room for the Gaekwar by the liberal use of old gold stain, which covered the walls and ceiling, with a dado improvised in rich tapestry.

In addition to fairy lights, illumination was provided by electricity. The Corporation Minute Book recorded that the electric light was 'steady and brilliant' from 8 p.m. to 5 a.m. The Minutes also recorded that the Gaekwar permitted the decorations and electric light to remain in place, free of charge, for a concert held in aid of local charities on 12 December.

Liberty's were by way of being

Above: *A drawing room designed and executed by Liberty & Co., 1906. This water colour also appears in the* Studio Yearbook of Decorative Art, *1906*

pioneers in the use of electric lighting, using it for their own Eastern Bazaar by 1887 and advertising that they could carry out schemes of electric lighting for both domestic and commercial use.

The only hitch in the proceedings occurred when one of Liberty's workmen accidentally damaged a picture, but Liberty's expressed their deep regret and offered to pay for the repair, an offer that was gratefully accepted.

The *Brighton Guardian* regarded the ball as 'the most splendid entertainment of its kind ever held in the Pavilion since it became the property of the Corporation'. This had been in 1850, when it was sold to the town by Queen Victoria for £53,000. To those who know the Pavilion today, the transformation must be hard to envisage, but when the

building was sold to the Corporation, most of the furniture and moveable decorative features were kept in Royal possession and dispersed, to be returned only in recent years.

The 1902 *Furniture* catalogue shows a wide range of Liberty furniture, including the 'Rowena' drawing room suite in mahogany. The cabinet from this suite, an example of which is now in the Cecil Higgins Museum, Bedford, was described as 'Mahogany cabinet, in rich colour with unvarnished surface. Relieved by three inlaid panels of various coloured woods and designed in the centre with a glazed cupboard for bric-à-brac. Suitable, also, for a boudoir'. The 'Ethelwynn' drawing room suite in walnut was somewhat simpler and showed something of an Austrian influ-

Above: *Oak dressing table inlaid with pewter and an oak washstand/chair from a bedroom suite, probably designed by Leonard Wyburd, c. 1899*

ence. The room setting for this suite showed a frieze probably designed by George Walton. The 'Helga' suite, described as 'a dainty bedroom suite in white enamelled wood', had a hanging wardrobe with a curtained space above for bonnets. The 'Athelstan' oak bedroom suite was shown in a room with a peacock frieze, and included the 'Stronza' armchair, an adaptation of a traditional Orkney chair with a high semi-circular back of woven rush. The 'Culloden' dining room suite was also included, another oak dining room suite called the 'Dunkeld' in which the wood was stained grey-brown and dull wax polished. This finish has recently been revived by Liberty in some reproductions of their turn of the century furniture.

The 1907 catalogue of furniture contains less of interest. Although the 'Culloden' and 'Athelstan' suites are still featured, the furniture on the whole is simpler and less original, with more or less straightforward reproductions or adaptations of 'Queen Anne' and 'Hepplewhite' furniture. Whether this was occasioned by the retirement of Leonard Wyburd in 1903, or merely by following the same path as Morris and Company and other high-class firms at that time, a distinct Liberty style is no longer dominant. There are a few touches of originality such as two charming swing cradles with embroidered linen curtains, illustrated in the *Studio Year Book of Decorative Art* (1906, p. 84), and a nursery dresser with inset pictorial panels of Dutch children. As a writer in the 1906 *Studio Year Book* wrote:

> . . . perhaps as a reaction to the extravagancies of art nouveau . . . the demand of the day . . . is practically confined to copies or adaptations of the past . . . It is not a little mortifying for all who have been looking hopefully . . . for a fresh and vital style in English furniture design, to be obliged to acknowledge that enterprise in that direction has sustained a check which has temporarily impeded its progress in that country.

Above: *Mahogany cabinet from the 'Rowena' drawing room suite, inlaid with stained woods, c. 1905*

This trend towards traditional design was to continue at Liberty's in the 1920s and 1930s, with most of the innovations in the field of textiles and dress. It was not until the 1950s that they were to resume their pioneering role in promoting the best of contemporary design, while successfully maintaining a traditional 'Liberty' image, a trend that has continued until the present day.

REFERENCE SECTION

COLLECTIONS

The museums and art galleries listed below contain collections of items made or sold by Liberty & Co. The list does not pretend to be comprehensive and many other museums have a few examples.

Great Britain

Victoria & Albert Museum, London: Textiles, wallpapers, original designs, silver, pewter, jewellery and metalwork, ceramics and glass, furniture and Far Eastern objects.

British Museum, London: Jewellery.

Worshipful Company of Goldsmiths, Goldsmiths' Hall, London: Silver.

Middlesex Polytechnic, Bounds Green, London: Silver Studio Collection.

Brighton Museum & Art Gallery: Furniture, silver and pewter.

City of Birmingham Museums & Art Galleries: Silver, jewellery and costume.

Platt Hall, Manchester: Costume.

Whitworth Art Gallery, Manchester: Textiles.
Sainsbury Centre, Norwich.

Anderson Collection of Art Nouveau.

Belgium

Musée Cinquantenaire, Brussels: Textiles

France

Musée de l'Impression sur Etoffes, Mulhouse: Textiles

Germany

Hessisches Landesmuseum, Darmstadt: Silver, pewter and jewellery

Museum für Kunst und Gewerbe, Hamburg: Textiles

Textilmuseum, Krefeld: Textiles

Norway

Nordenfjeldske Kunstindustrimuseum, Trondheim: Furniture, textiles, silver and pewter

Sweden

Nordiska Museet, Stockholm: Textiles

U.S.A.

Metropolitan Museum of Art, New York: Costume

Museum of Modern Art, New York: Objects by Archibald Knox and Christopher Dresser.

BIBLIOGRAPHY

Contemporary Sources and Periodicals

Artist, 1880–1902
Art et Décoration (Paris) 1897–1914
Architectural Review, 1896–
Der Moderne Stil (Stuttgart) 1899–1905
Deutsche Kunst und Decoration (Darmstadt) 1897–1934
Liberty Catalogues (in the Victoria & Albert Museum National Art Library)
Liberty Lamp (house magazine), February 1925–January 1932
Magazine of Art 1878–1904
Studio 1893–
Studio. Special Winter Number: Jewellery and Fans, 1901–2
Studio Year Book of Decorative Art, 1906–29

Recent sources

Adburgham, Alison, *Liberty's: A biography of a shop*, London, 1975
Aslin, Elizabeth. *19th Century English Furniture*, London, 1962
Aslin, Elizabeth. *The Aesthetic Movement*, London, 1969
Aslin, Elizabeth. *E.W. Godwin. Furniture and Interior Decoration*, London, 1986

Bury, Shirley. 'The Liberty Metalwork Venture'. *Architectural Review*, February 1963, p. 108–111
Bury, Shirley. 'New Light on the Liberty Metalwork Venture'. *Journal of the Decorative Art Society*, vol. I, p. 14–27
Cooper, Jeremy. *Victorian and Edwardian Furniture and Interiors*, London, 1987
Crawford, Alan. *C.R. Ashbee. Architect, Designer and Romantic Socialist.* New Haven and London, 1985.
Levy, Mervyn. *Liberty Style. The Classic Years: 1898–1910.* London, 1986
Liberty's 1875–1975. Catalogue of an Exhibition to Mark the Firm's Centenary. HMSO, London, 1975
Parry, Linda. *Textiles of the Arts & Crafts Movement.* London, 1988
Tilbrook, Adrian J. (jointly edited with Gordon House). *The Designs of Archibald Knox for Liberty & Co.* Ornament Press, London, 1976
Turner, Mark. *The Silver Studio Collection. A London Design Studio 1880–1963.* London, 1980
Turner, Mark. *Art Nouveau Designs from the Silver Studio Collection.* London, 1986
Turner, Mark, and Hoskins, Lesley. *Silver Studio of Design.* London, 1988
Walkling, Gillian. *Antique Bamboo Furniture.* London, 1979

INDEX

Page number in *italic* refer to the illustrations

ACKNOWLEDGEMENTS

The research carried out by my former colleagues in connection with the 1975 Liberty Centenary Exhibition at the Victoria & Albert Museum has formed a sound basis for much of the material in this book. I am particularly indebted to Elizabeth Aslin for information on Liberty furniture, to Shirley Bury for information on silver and jewellery, and to David Coachworth for his research on pewter and ceramics. I was also closely involved with the exhibition and, together with Valerie Mendes, was responsible for the textiles, embroideries and carpets.

My thanks are also due to Widar Halén for information on Christopher Dresser's involvement with Liberty's, to Mark Turner for his work on the Silver Studio, and especially to Peter Rose and Albert Gallichan for allowing me to make use of both objects and documentation in their collection.

I would also like to express my thanks to the staff of numerous museums, both at home and abroad, and to dealers and auction houses, for making photographs available.

Finally, my grateful thanks go to Brenda Spooner for typing my manuscript so accurately and speedily.

BARBARA MORRIS.
December, 1988.